Living ha

Childr
low-in...

Rebecca O'Connell, Abigail Knight and Julia Brannen

CPAG • 30 Micawber Street • London N1 7TB

Child Poverty Action Group works on behalf of the more than one in four children in the UK growing up in poverty. It doesn't have to be like this. We use our understanding of what causes poverty and the impact it has on children's lives to campaign for policies that will prevent and solve poverty – for good. We provide training, advice and information to make sure hard-up families get the financial support they need. We also carry out high profile legal work to establish and protect families' rights.

The views expressed are those of the authors and do not necessarily represent the views of the Child Poverty Action Group.

30 Micawber Street
London N1 7TB
Tel: 020 7837 7979
staff@cpag.org.uk
www.cpag.org.uk

© Child Poverty Action Group 2019

This book is sold subject to the condition that it shall not, by way of trade or otherwise, be lent, resold, hired out or otherwise circulated without the publisher's prior consent in any form of binding or cover other than that in which it is published and without a similar condition including this condition being imposed on the subsequent purchaser.

A CIP record for this book is available from the British Library

ISBN: 978 1 910715 47 5
Child Poverty Action Group is a charity registered in England and Wales (registration number 294841) and in Scotland (registration number SC039339), and is a company limited by guarantee, registered in England (registration number 1993854). VAT number: 690 808117

Cover design by Colorido Studios
Cover illustration by sketchpadstudio.com
Typeset by Devious Designs
Printed and bound in the UK by CPI Group (UK) Ltd

Acknowledgements

First and foremost, the authors would wish to thank the young people and their families who participated in the study. Thanks also to the UK and international research team, the research advisory group and the European Research Council for funding the study. The research leading to these results has received funding from the European Research Council under the European Union's Seventh Framework Programme (FP7/2007-2013), ERC grant agreement number 337977. Funding for the book has been gratefully received from UCL Innovation and Enterprise's Knowledge Exchange and Innovation Fund, supported by HEIF.

We are very grateful for the enthusiasm and commitment of all those who have contributed time and energy to this book. We are especially indebted to Liz Dowler for her expert guidance and to Jonathan Bradshaw, Alan Marsh and Ruth Wright for their valued comments on the draft. Thanks are due to Nicola Johnston for editing and managing the production, Kathleen Armstrong for proofreading, and to Alison Garnham, Louisa McGeehan, Moussa Haddad, Lizzie Flew and other CPAG staff for their guidance. Special thanks to our colleagues at the Thomas Coram Research Unit for their support and to Alanna Ivin for her careful transcription of the interviews.

For the children in the study
and in loving memory of Douglas Michael Wright
(28 May 2013 –15 February 2018)

About the authors

Rebecca O'Connell is a reader in the sociology of food and families at the Thomas Coram Research Unit, University College London (UCL) Institute of Education. She is co-author, with Julia Brannen, of *Food, Families, and Work* (2016) and principal investigator of the European Research Council funded study, *Families and Food in Hard Times*.

Abigail Knight is a lecturer in sociology at the Thomas Coram Research Unit, UCL Institute of Education. As well as teaching, she is a qualitative researcher with children and families and has researched and written widely on the lives of young people in care, children with disabilities and families living in poverty.

Julia Brannen is professor of the sociology of the family at the Thomas Coram Research Unit, UCL Institute of Education and fellow of the Academy of Social Science. She has an international reputation for research on methodology, the lives of children and young people in families, work-family life and intergenerational relationships. Recent books include *Fathers and Sons* (2015) and *Practising Social Research* (forthcoming Policy Press).

Contents

Foreword

Louise Tickle
Education and social affairs journalist and
Orwell Fellow

Every parent wants to feed their child. The drive to provide food for your baby is an overwhelming human instinct: hearing a toddler wailing 'I'm hungry!' is exquisitely painful to any mother or father who hears the cry.

But what if there's no milk, no bread, no baked beans, no cheese, no fish fingers, no peanut butter, no tuna, no fresh veg, no tomato sauce, no apples, no bananas, absolutely nothing in the cupboard – because there's no money to make a trip to the shop?

This book details, often in their own words, the lives of children whose parents can't afford to put regular meals on the table. There are far too many of them: over four million children in one of the richest countries in the world are growing up in poverty, their access to adequate nutrition compromised.

As an education reporter, in recent years it has become ever more apparent that teachers are worried about hungry pupils who can't concentrate: their education suffers. Children in this book talk about their shame at being on free school dinners, which affects relationships in their friendship groups, and can also lead to bullying. One mother in the book talks about not eating for four days: it's heartbreaking to then hear the mounting anxiety children describe for a parent who is choosing to skip meals in order that they may eat. The guilt at what their parents are enduring is a burden no young person should have to bear.

While children arrive at school without breakfast, and later do their homework fuelled by nothing but a piece of toast, commentators are busy talking about various manifestations of poverty – housing poverty, period poverty, transport poverty, fuel poverty – but in the end, these are just different ways of saying the same thing: families are now struggling to give their children a decent start because there is not enough money to afford the basics.

Food banks are not the answer. Those who work in them acknowledge they are barely a sticking plaster. From the perspective of an alien arriving from outer space – or even a visitor from a country with a functional social contract – these warehouses of tinned and dried foodstuffs must appear similar in their operation to the way ravenous people in conflict-riven areas are kept from tipping into starvation by distributions of humanitarian aid.

That addressing 'holiday hunger' is also now a regular aspect of many charities' work is also a burning indictment of a society unable to ensure families have sufficient income to keep their children safe, secure and nourished.

Food is so much more than just the building blocks that children need to survive. Good food is fundamental to culture; it is a cornerstone of building community; it is about being able to take part in social activities with your friends. These are not added extras; they are central to a good life. Food, ultimately, is about how well humans can thrive. And brutally, it comes down to this: in the UK, in 2019, children's lives are being blighted and their life chances curtailed because they are not getting what they need to eat.

One
Introduction

Food is fundamental. It is essential to physical survival, a medium for the expression of identity and central to a sense of belonging. Food therefore provides a revealing lens for understanding how poverty and low income affect the lives of children and their families. Through the stories of children in 45 families, this book examines the reasons children go without decent food and what they say about being excluded from eating in ways that are customary in Britain today.

From *Poverty Bites* to *Living Hand to Mouth*

In 1999, the then Prime Minister, Tony Blair, pledged to end child poverty in the UK within 20 years. Two years later, CPAG published *Poverty Bites: food, health and poor families* which explored the consequences for low-income families struggling to afford sufficient food to maintain good health in terms of their nutritional, health and social wellbeing.[1] So, 20 years after the pledge to end child poverty, why are we still talking about food poverty within families with children?

During the 1997–2010 Labour administration, the task to end child poverty started well. Welfare benefits, particularly for children, were increased and more help was given to raise earned income among families living in poverty and improve children's services.[2] Child poverty rates fell significantly. Since then, however, the situation has seriously deteriorated. It is scarcely believable that the words of Maud Pember Reeves, written over a hundred years ago, need repeating today:[3]

> It is to the collective interest of a nation that its children should flourish.
>
> There should be no such thing as an underfed school child: an underfed child is a disgrace and a danger to the state.

By 2012, the UK Poverty and Social Exclusion study suggested that well over half a million children lived in families who could not afford to feed them properly.[4] Parents were unable to provide at least one of the following:

three meals a day; daily fresh fruit and vegetables; or meat, fish or a vegetarian equivalent at least once a day. It found that if many parents were not cutting back on their own food intake to protect their children, the number of children going without would be much higher.

In the UK, one of the richest countries in the world, the outlook for children in low-income families is currently bleak. Child poverty targets have been scrapped and poverty rates are rising. By 2021, five million children will be living in relative income poverty – that is, below 60 per cent of average (median) income.

Children, food and poverty

As Peter Townsend made clear, poverty is about more than low income.[5] In the UK, households with children are currently more likely to be living in poverty than any other household type.[6] Yet, we know very little about how children and young people living in different kinds of families negotiate food and eating in conditions of disadvantage and inequality. It is in the context of what has been called 'breadline Britain'[7] that this book returns to the fundamental issue of food in low-income families. It especially seeks to understand the problem from children's perspectives.

Food is fundamental to children's lives and to their physical, emotional and mental health as growing individuals. The harmful consequences of poor diet intake and malnutrition, particularly for children, are well established and have long-term implications. These include the increasing incidence of coronary heart disease, type II diabetes and cancer.[8] Indeed, the UK Faculty of Public Health argues that the recent evidence of increasing malnutrition constitutes a 'public health emergency'.[9] Health and dietary inequalities in the UK are linked to inequalities in income: 11–15-year-olds in less affluent families in England report less healthy eating, including lower consumption of fruit and vegetables, than those from more affluent families.[10] In the UK, as elsewhere, poverty is also closely connected to being overweight and obesity,[11] a trend partly explained by the relative cheapness and wide availability of unhealthy foods that are high in saturated fat and added sugars.[12] Suboptimal diets and food habits such as skipping meals are also associated with poor cognition and lower academic achievement as children's ability to concentrate is damaged by insufficient food or food of low nutritious value.[13]

'Sometimes you don't have enough energy, you cannot cope in the class-room so you have to, like, try and rest a bit. You just put your head on the table and you end up falling asleep in the classroom and you get in trouble for it.' (Emmanuel, age 14, does not have anything to eat during the school day)

Food is also vital to children's participation in society. It is an important lens for understanding lived experiences of both material deprivation and social exclusion. Eating with others plays a significant role in establishing and cementing social networks, with food mediating children's attempts to make friends and connect with others.[14] Food is also integral to the reciprocal relationships of care in which children – and adults – are enmeshed.[15] It is a medium for children's expression of identity and control and, in a consumerised culture, choosing what food to buy and eat is a means of enacting increasing autonomy as they grow older.[16] Exclusion from the eating activities that form part of children's and young people's 'ordinary living patterns'[17] may therefore be regarded as a dimension of relative poverty.[18]

'I don't want to show them that, no, I don't have enough money. I say to them "no I don't really want to come".' (Faith, age 15, on being invited to the cinema and for something to eat with her friends)

Living Hand to Mouth is about children who are at significant risk of food poverty. It adopts a contextual approach that puts a spotlight on the material realities of children's and young people's lives in Britain today: what it means to live in low-income households that have constrained budgets, especially concerning access to food. It examines children's accounts of their everyday experiences and the social, geographical and economic conditions in which they live.

The study

The book is based on a study of 51 children, from 45 families, in two areas of South East England that, given this is the richest region of Britain, increases the gap between rich and poor.[19] It focuses on children's experiences of food in different settings: at home, in school and out of school. The book also includes photographs of food taken by some of the children. These illustrate something of the diversity of the children's backgrounds, the kinds of food they selected and those that were available to them. Participants were given good-quality digital cameras to use and keep but, nonetheless, not all their photographs are of usual print quality. However, we felt strongly it was important to include them.

The book sets children's accounts in the context of what we also learned from interviews with their parents. It locates the children in the neighbourhoods where they meet their peers and in schools, in particular their experiences of school meals. It recounts how children felt about, and managed, the experience of poverty in general and of being seen to be 'poor' as they compare themselves with peers in a highly consumerist society. Finally, it addresses who children hold responsible for ensuring, or failing to ensure, that they have enough to eat.

> 'If a child dies the government is always serious about it. So, if the child doesn't die, they should still be serious about the child anyway.' (Ayo, age 12, West African, inner London)

The chapters

Chapter 2 sets out the political, economic and social policy contexts, particularly as they affect the money people have for everyday living. It examines the implications for living and food standards, including evidence about rising levels of food poverty in Britain considering the impact of austerity for families. Chapter 3 describes the conceptual approaches

Onions are 'the only thing that lasts', says Bryony's mother. Her partner says: 'Sometimes when we've got more money there'd be potatoes in there, there'd be parsnips, extra stuff.'

Fahad said this is 'just an average dinner': 'pasta, sweetcorn, salt and pepper and some mince'.

adopted in the book. It sets ways of thinking about food and poverty in historical context, before describing our approach to understanding children's and families' lives.

Chapter 4 describes the study and the children's families on which the book is based. In Chapter 5, we examine what food poverty is for the study families, in particular how far they go without proper food and how they get by. We consider the variation among the sample in terms not only of the quantity of food available but also its quality. More importantly, given that the book is about children living in low-income families, we examine their experiences. This has involved taking a close look at their own accounts, and those of their parents, about what they eat. Key to understanding how children were affected is parental sacrifice: how far it was possible for parents to protect children from going hungry or going without food. We show that some parents successfully protected children while others could not and we examine the methods they used to get by and the conditions under which this occurred.

Chapter 6 addresses the food children eat in school. It begins by describing children's experiences in the schools they attended, before examining the place of school meals in the lives of these young people in low-income families through cases of children who are entitled to free school meals and those who are not. A crucial dimension of this analysis is the school's policy: whether the school adopts an inclusive approach towards school meals and free school meals irrespective of financial constraints and formal regulations on them, or whether the approach is exclusionary.

Chapter 7 focuses on children's opportunities for, and experiences of, participation and social inclusion with regard to food and eating. As 'eating the same food as others is a basic mark of belonging',[20] children's social lives can be significantly restricted when resources are constrained, leading to fewer opportunities for social participation and social inclusion. We consider how far young people were able to join in with their peers outside of school and home, when buying snacks and meals in their neighbourhoods – from shops and cafes after school and at weekends – whether they were able to socialise with peers in each other's homes and the constraints and capabilities of the different study areas.

In Chapter 8, we focus on children's own accounts of food poverty, poverty in general and being seen to be 'poor'. In a highly consumerist society children may see that money is a source of worry for their parents while they may experience shame as they compare themselves with peers. In the second part of the chapter, we consider what children say when asked who they hold responsible for ensuring, or not ensuring, that children have enough to eat.

Chapter 9 summarises the study's findings and considers recommendations for what might be done to ensure young people and their families have access to adequate food for health and social participation.

Notes

1   E Dowler, S Turner and B Dobson, *Poverty Bites: food, health and poor families,* Child Poverty Action Group, 2001

2   Child Poverty Action Group, *Ending Child Poverty by 2020: progress made and lessons learned*, 2012

3   M Pember Reeves, *Round about a Pound a Week,* Persephone Books, 1913, p227 and p229

4   D Gordon and others, *The Impoverishment of the UK: PSE UK first results: living standards*, PSE UK, 2013

5   P Townsend, *Poverty in the United Kingdom: a survey of household resources and standards of living*, Allen Lane and Penguin Books, 1979

6   A Marsh, K Barker, C Ayrton, M Treanor and M Haddad, *Poverty: the facts*, Child Poverty Action Group, 2017, pp116–17

7   S Lansley and J Mack, *Breadline Britain: the rise of mass poverty*, Oneworld Publications, 2015

8   J Mack, 'Child maltreatment and child mortality' in V Cooper and D Whyte (eds), *The Violence of Austerity,* Pluto Press, 2017; Royal College of Paediatrics and Child Health and Child Poverty Action Group, *Poverty and Child Health: views from the frontline*, Royal College of Paediatrics and Child Health, 2017; SI Kirk-

patrick, L McIntyre and ML Potestio, 'Child hunger and long-term adverse consequences for health', *Archives of Pediatrics and Adolescent Medicine*, 164(8), 2010, pp754–62

9 JR Ashton, J Middleton and T Lang, 'Open letter to Prime Minister David Cameron on food poverty in the UK', *The Lancet*, 383(9929), 2014, p1631

10 A Simon, C Owen, R O'Connell and F Brooks, 'Changing trends in young people's food behaviour and wellbeing in England in relation to family affluence between 2005 and 2014', *Journal of Youth Studies,* 21(5), 2018, pp687–700

11 House of Commons Health Committee, *Childhood Obesity: time for action, eighth report of session 2017–19*, 2018; S Kinra, RP Nelder and GJ Lewendon, 'Deprivation and childhood obesity: a cross sectional study of 20,973 children in Plymouth, United Kingdom', *Journal of Epidemiology and Community Health*, 54(6), 2000, pp456–60

12 S Vandevijvere and others, 'Increased food energy supply as a major driver of the obesity epidemic: a global analysis', *Bulletin of the World Health Organization*, 2013, 93(7), pp446–56

13 A Hoyland, L Dye and C Lawton, 'A systematic review of the effect of breakfast on the cognitive performance of children and adolescents', *Nutritional Research Reviews*, 22(2), 2009, pp220–43

14 A James, 'Confections, concoctions and conceptions', *Journal of the Anthropological Society of Oxford*, 10(2), 1979, pp83–95

15 G Clement, *Care, Autonomy, and Justice: feminism and the ethic of care,* Westview, 1996; D Cook, 'The missing child in consumption theory', *Journal of Consumer Culture*, 8(2), 2008, pp219–43

16 R O'Connell and J Brannen, *Food, Families and Work*, Bloomsbury, 2016

17 See note 5

18 R O'Connell, C Owen, M Padley, A Simon and J Brannen, 'Which types of family are at risk of food poverty in the UK? A relative deprivation approach', *Social Policy and Society,* 5 February 2018, pp1–18

19 The book focuses on families living in England as one part of the UK, made up of Scotland, England, Wales and Northern Ireland. Since 1999, some of the UK's powers, in areas that include health and education, have been devolved to assemblies in Cardiff and Belfast and the Scottish Parliament in Edinburgh. The experiences of children and families in relation to food and eating that are explored in the book are, therefore, situated in an English policy context, although we also refer to social trends pertinent to food poverty across the UK as a whole.

20 D Stone, *Policy Paradox and Political Reason*, Scott Foresman and Company, 1988, p71

Two
Food poverty in Britain

Food poverty, widely defined as 'the inability to acquire or consume an adequate quality or sufficient quantity of food in socially acceptable ways, or the uncertainty that one will be able to do so',[1] has become a major moral and social concern in Britain.[2]

The combined effects of economic recession and welfare retrenchment in the aftermath of the 2008 global financial crisis have had a profound effect on many European countries. They have led to a significant decline in household incomes and, increasingly, vulnerability to poverty.[3] This is especially true in the UK where 'an unprecedented squeeze' on the growth of average or median wages followed the financial crisis.[4] The Institute for Fiscal Studies found that between 2008 and 2015 median 'real' earnings (what wages are worth after adjusting for inflation) remained stagnant or fell. Income from employment was on average still lower than before the recession in the UK.[5]

Under the guise of deficit reduction, so-called 'austerity' measures from 2010 have also hit many British people hard. Deep welfare retrenchment, following the Welfare Reform Act 2012, has introduced progressively harsher cuts to welfare spending such as the freezing of child benefit for four years and the introduction of a 'benefit cap' on the overall value of benefits a family can receive, including a limit to the amount of housing benefit that can be claimed despite rising rents. Under this Act, the introduction of the under-occupancy penalty (known as the 'bedroom tax'), the implementation of universal credit and an increasingly restricted access to employment and support allowance for disabled people have produced much controversy. More recently, in April 2017, the 'two-child limit' on the child elements of child tax credit and universal credit came into effect. This policy discriminates against larger families and severs the link between need and support that is the foundation of a 'just and compassionate welfare state'.[6]

Austerity policies such as these have not only reduced some people's incomes considerably, but also changed the normative expectations of the post-war welfare state, both in terms of what 'social security' is meant to provide and how society regards those who need to use the benefits system. In addition, obtaining benefits has been made much more difficult and the administration is punitive. Sanctions – a regime of docking benefits as punishment for alleged failures to comply with job centre rules – have been found to be ineffective at getting jobless people into work and are more likely to increase poverty, food bank use, illhealth and crime.[7]

Despite the ideological mantra that 'work pays',[8] the largest proportion of households with children living in relative poverty in the UK includes at least one employed adult.[9] The deregulation of the labour market has resulted in the growth of precarious employment, including zero-hour contracts. Such conditions engender insecurity and considerable anxiety for workers about 'making ends meet' and providing adequately for themselves and their families.[10] In this context, debt has become pervasive and normal, taking the place of a living wage and sufficient welfare provisions.[11] Many households use credit to pay for basic living costs and high levels of 'problem debt' are commonplace, causing distress and vulnerability to economic shocks.[12] The Institute of Fiscal Studies recently found that around a quarter of the lowest income households are struggling with arrears or high debt repayments.[13]

The consequences of austerity policies have included rising levels of relative poverty particularly among families with children.[14] The number of children in poverty has risen by 500,000, from 3.6 million in 2010–2012, to 4.1 million in 2016–2017.[15] That's 30 per cent of children, or nine in a classroom of 30.[16] The UK, which has had a poor record on child poverty compared to other similarly developed countries, has fallen further behind. According to Eurostat 2014, over 22 per cent of UK children lived in materially deprived households (that is, they went without three or more essential items) compared to 14 per cent in France, 12 per cent in Germany and 4 per cent in Norway and Sweden.[17] The association between being born into families experiencing poverty and deprivation and high rates of poor health outcomes in later life is well established.[18] As we discuss below, food and nutrition play a fundamental role.

Living and food standards

As a result of the fall in real incomes from earnings since 2008 and benefits from 2010, people in the UK have encountered falling living standards; that is, the cost of necessities, including food, has outstripped the money available for them. The impacts have not been distributed evenly.[19] Low-income households have been disproportionately affected by the rising price of essentials such as housing, domestic utilities and food, which have increased faster than consumer prices more generally.[20] Spending on food is a large proportion of household expenditure for the poorest families with the result that it has become less affordable. In 2015/16, the proportion of spending on food and non-alcoholic drinks for the average UK household was 10.7 per cent, while for households with the lowest 20 per cent of income it was higher, at 16 per cent.[21]

Since the food budget may be relatively 'elastic' compared to other essential living costs that have also risen over the last decade, people can – and do – cut back on food to meet competing demands. Research shows that healthier foods are more expensive than those that are less healthy;[22] households seeking to economise may 'trade down' to cheaper versions of the same products or change what they buy and consume. During the 2008 recession, there was a decline in the average nutritional quality of foods purchased, driven primarily by substitution towards processed food and away from fruit and vegetables. The largest switches away from fruit and vegetables were by households with young children and lone-parent households.[23] In 2012, those in the lowest income decile spent 22 per cent more on food than in 2007 and purchased 5.7 per cent less, buying significantly fewer portions of fruit and vegetables than previously.[24] As Liz Dowler notes, however, those on the very lowest incomes do not trade down 'because they have less opportunity to do so, being already on the most basic of diets'.[25] The ways in which families try to manage include borrowing money, juggling bills and accessing free food from food banks, access to which is usually through a referral from a 'front-line professional' such as a GP, social worker or Citizens Advice.[26]

Charlie's pasta with salt. When asked whether he ever had it with anything on it – such as oil or butter – he said he did but there was neither. 'On this day, there was like nothing left in the house apart from pasta.'

Between 2010/11 and 2016/17, the number of food parcels the Trussell Trust food bank network provided grew from about 61,500 to over 1.18 million.[27] Research examining the reasons for this explosion finds an association with welfare reform; benefit sanctions and delays are the most commonly cited reason for food bank referral alongside recent loss of earnings or changes in family circumstances.[28] However, food-insecure households do not necessarily use food banks, as evidence from Canada suggests that people may not want to receive charity or do not have access to food banks.[29] Moreover, food banks do not primarily serve those in chronic poverty who struggle every day to put food on the table but rather those whose inadequate incomes make them vulnerable to acute crises.[30] See, for example, Amara's case on p42.

In the UK, no government department has responsibility for measuring and monitoring household food poverty or insecurity and there is no 'official' definition of either. However, a recent survey by the Food Standards Agency[31] found that 8 per cent of adults were classed as having moderate or severe levels of food insecurity, defined in this survey as not having access at all times to enough food that is both sufficiently varied and culturally appropriate to sustain an active and healthy life.[32] Adults with incomes in the bottom quartile, adults who were unemployed or economically inactive, and adults who were under 35 years of age were significantly most likely to be food insecure. But food insecurity also affected adults in work; about 7 per cent were moderately or severely food insecure. The survey only asked about adults' experiences and not those of children.

Families and food poverty

Families with children have been hit hard by austerity and some suffer more than others.[33] Since 2010, lone parents in the lowest 20 per cent of the income distribution have lost 8 per cent of real income, couples with children about 11 per cent.[34] This income loss is reflected in rising levels of food poverty and demand for emergency food aid. The provision of food parcels to households with children by food banks has grown considerably since the introduction of welfare reform, austerity measures and fluctuating living costs.[35] While food banks have become a symbol for food poverty in 'breadline Britain', reports in the mainstream media fail to reflect the experiences of families or children. Indeed, little attention is paid to those who manage to get by without recourse to food banks, perhaps by turning to friends and family, or those who live in ever-increasing debt.[36]

Research based on the Joseph Rowntree Foundation's Minimum Income Standard (MIS) found that large families (households with three or more children) and lone-parent families are most likely to struggle to meet the budget standard for a socially acceptable, healthy diet and be at risk of food poverty.[37] Lone-parent households are also the largest proportion of households helped by the Trussell Trust food banks and children living in large families are over-represented.[38] These findings suggest that food poverty, like income poverty, is not evenly distributed.

Yet we know little about how children and young people living in different types of family experience and think about food poverty or how they negotiate food and eating in conditions of disadvantage and inequality. Research focusing specifically on food poverty among children in the UK is limited, small scale and has generally been carried out by non-governmental organisations.[39] Studies that consider families' experiences of food poverty suggest that some parents (particularly mothers) in low-income households skip meals at times to protect their children from going without and that some children also skip meals or report going to bed hungry.[40] In addition, for many low-income families, it is difficult for children to invite friends home for a meal.[41] Research also suggests that some children, particularly those who receive free school meals, experience 'holiday hunger',[42] an issue that has recently been taken up by local authorities, charities, politicians and the media.[43]

The role of the state and school food

In the UK context, in which there is a neoliberal emphasis on individual responsibility for health,[44] a body that oversees policy that could address the food and nutritional needs of low-income households is long overdue.[45] Anti-poverty measures aimed at children and their families have been marked by the tension between the interests of the state and the rights and responsibilities of parents.[46] Given longstanding political concerns in the UK about 'state interference in the private realm of the family and the abdication of parental responsibility', historically school meals have largely been framed in health and educational terms rather than as a welfare intervention.[47]

For more than a century, the government has provided free school meals (FSMs) to children whose education might otherwise suffer. In England, *the School Food Plan* – a review of school food under the Coalition government – universally rolled out FSMs to all Key Stage 1 children with the aim 'to improve academic attainment and save families money'.[48]

For older children at state schools, FSM eligibility is linked to the parent (or the young person) being in receipt of certain means-tested benefits.[49] However, it has been calculated that around a third of pupils living below the poverty line are not eligible for FSMs because their parents are not on 'out-of-work' benefits.[50] For example, working tax credit – paid to low-paid workers employed for at least 16 hours a week – is not an eligible benefit. Also, the universal credit earnings limit introduced from April 2018 means that, in England, children in low-income families with a net income of more than £7,400 a year are ineligible for FSMs. This has led some to argue that it fundamentally undermines one of the main reasons for introducing universal credit in the first place: to ensure that 'work always pays'.[51] As the qualifying benefits for FSMs are public funds, it also means that FSMs cannot be claimed by people with 'no recourse to public funds'.

In addition to eligibility issues, research identifies problems with the adequacy and delivery of FSMs.[52] Highlighting the insufficiency of FSM allowances, research by CPAG and the British Youth Council found that one in seven young people indicated that their FSM allowance did not allow them to purchase a full meal.[53] The research also found that delivery systems could be stigmatising. To be identified as receiving FSMs is to be identified as being 'poor' by peers, leading in some cases to feelings of shame and embarrassment and to bullying. This included being identified by payment systems and having to queue and eat separately, which meant exclusion from the 'normal' lunchtime experience of 'hanging out' with friends.[54] While new cashless systems since introduced in many schools play a part in preventing identification of children on FSMs, as our study found, children may still be identified and discriminated against, for example, through the different foods available to them.

> 'It's embarrassing, yeah, you have no money on your card and then you just watch them eat.' (Gideon, age 15, on not having enough money to buy a school lunch)

The school setting is significant in terms of its contribution to overall diet and eating practices. It has been estimated that young people consume around a third of their food and drink during the school day.[55] The School Food Standards introduced in England in 2015 endorse a 'whole school approach' to healthy school meals that has been shown to play a role in improvements in academic attainment.[56] However, the standards are not mandatory for all schools and research suggests patchy implementation as well as contradictions between the curriculum and the availability of nutritious food in schools.[57]

While the *School Food Plan* states that eating in school should be pleasurable, this has been neglected by policymakers overwhelmingly concerned with nutrition. Schools have, therefore, been criticised for focusing on what children put in their mouths at the expense of addressing the context where food is consumed.[58] However, research has long suggested the importance of the social dimensions of eating in school from children's points of view,[59] not least because when children's perspectives are taken into account they are more likely to eat the food on offer.

Notes

1   E Dowler, S Turner and B Dobson, *Poverty Bites: food, health and poor families*, Child Poverty Action Group, 2001, p2

2   E Dowler and D O'Connor, 'Rights-based approaches to addressing food poverty and food insecurity in Ireland and UK', *Social Science and Medicine*, 74(1), 2012, pp44–51; E Dowler, 'Food Banks and Food Justice in "Austerity Britain"', in G Riches and T Silvasti (eds), *First World Hunger Revisited: food charity or the right to food?*, Palgrave Macmillan, 2014, pp160–75

3   D Matsaganis and C Levanti, 'The distributional effect of austerity and the recession in Southern Europe', *Southern European Society and Politics* 19(3), 2014, pp393–412

4   S Clare and C D'Arcy, *Low Pay Britain 2016*, Resolution Foundation, 2016

5   C Belfield, J Cribb, A Hood and R Joyce, *Living Standards, Poverty and Inequality in the UK: 2016*, Institute for Fiscal Studies, 2016, p14

6   T Sefton and J Tucker, *Unhappy Birthday! The two-child limit at one year old*, End Child Poverty, 2018

7   Welfare Conditionality Project, *Final Findings Report: welfare conditionality project 2013–18*, available at www.welfareconditionality.ac.uk/publications/final-findings-report

8   V Cooper and D Whyte (eds), *The Violence of Austerity*, Pluto Press, 2017, p12

9   R Hick and A Lanau, *In-work Poverty in the UK: problem, policy analysis and platform for action*, Nuffield Foundation, 2017

10 K Newsome, J Heyes, S Moore, D Smith and M Tomlinson, *Living on the Edge: experiencing workplace insecurity in the UK*, Trades Union Congress, 2018, p7

11 D Ellis, 'The Violence of the Debtfare State', in V Cooper and D Whyte (eds), *The Violence of Austerity*, Pluto Press, 2017, pp110–16

12 S Mahony and L Pople, *Life in the Debt Trap: stories of children and families struggling with debt*, Policy Press, 2018

13 A Hood, R Joyce and D Sturrock, *Problem Debt and Low-income Households*, Institute for Fiscal Studies, 2018

14 J Mack, 'Child maltreatment and child mortality', in V Cooper and D Whyte

(eds), *The Violence of Austerity,* Pluto Press, 2017, pp85–93

15 Department for Work and Pensions, *Households Below Average Income, Statistics on the number and percentage of people living in low income households for financial years 1994/95 to 2016/17*, Tables 4a and 4b, 2018

16 www.cpag.org.uk/content/child-poverty-facts-and-figures

17 See note 14

18 J Bradshaw (ed), *The Well-being of Children in the United Kingdom*, Policy Press, 2011; J Tucker (ed), *Improving Children's Life Chances*, Child Poverty Action Group, 2016

19 A Davis and M Padley, 'What the minimum income standard tells us about living standards in the United Kingdom', in D Fee and A Kober-Smith (eds), *Inequalities in the UK: new discourses, evolutions and actions,* Emerald Publishing, 2017

20 T MacInnes and others, *Monitoring Poverty and Social Exclusion 2015*, Joseph Rowntree Foundation, 2015, p20

21 Department for Environment, Food and Rural Affairs, *Family Food 2016/17: expenditure*, 2018

22 NRV Jones, AI Conklin, M Suhrcke and P Monsivais, 'The growing price gap between more and less healthy foods: analysis of a novel longitudinal UK dataset', *PLoS One*, 9(10), 2014, e109343

23 R Griffith, M O'Connell and K Smith, *Food Expenditure and Nutritional Quality over the Great Recession*, Institute for Fiscal Studies, 2013

24 Department for Environment, Food and Rural Affairs, *Food Statistics Pocketbook 2012*, 2013

25 E Dowler, 'Food banks and food justice in "Austerity Britain"', in G Riches and T Silvasti (eds), *First World Hunger Revisited: food charity or the right to food?*, Palgrave Macmillan, 2014, pp160–75

26 H Lambie-Mumford, *The Right to Food and the Rise of Charitable Emergency Food Provision in the United Kingdom*, PhD thesis, Department of Geography, University of Sheffield, 2014, p66

27 The Trussell Trust, 'UK foodbank use continues to rise as new report highlights growing impact of universal credit rollout on foodbanks', 25 April 2017, blog post available at www.trusselltrust.org/2017/04/25/uk-foodbank-use-continues-rise

28 J Perry, M Williams, T Sefton and M Haddad, *Emergency Use Only: understanding and reducing the use of food banks in the UK*, Child Poverty Action Group, Church of England, Oxfam GB and The Trussell Trust, 2014

29 R Loopstra and V Tarasuk, 'Food bank usage is a poor indicator of food insecurity: insights from Canada', *Social Policy and Society*, 14(3), 2015, pp443–55

30 R Loopstra and D Lalor, *Financial Insecurity, Food Insecurity, and Disability: the profile of people receiving emergency food assistance from The Trussell Trust Foodbank Network in Britain,* The Trussell Trust, 2017, p2

31 B Bates, C Roberts, H Lepps and L Porter, *The Food and You Survey Wave 4,*

Food Standards Agency, 2017

32 International agencies, including the United Nations, and some other countries such as the United States and Canada, use the term 'food insecurity' as a way of conceptualising and measuring food poverty.

33 See note 14

34 A Marsh with K Barker, C Ayrton, M Treanor and M Haddad, *Poverty: the facts*, 6th Edition, Child Poverty Action Group, 2017

35 H Lambie-Mumford and M Green, 'Austerity, welfare reform and the rising use of food banks by children in England and Wales', *Area* 49(3), 2015, pp273–79

36 A Knight, R O'Connell and J Brannen, 'Eating with friends, family or not at all: young people's experiences of food poverty in the UK', in W Wills and R O'Connell (eds), *Children and Society*, Special issue: 'Children's and young people's food practices in contexts of poverty and inequality', 32(3), 2018, pp244–54

37 R O'Connell, C Owen, M Padley, A Simon and J Brannen, 'Which types of family are at risk of food poverty in the UK? A relative deprivation approach', *Social Policy and Society,* 5 February 2018, available at https://doi.org/10.1017/S1474746418000015

38 See note 30

39 For example, K Harvey, *Children and Parents' Experiences of Food Insecurity in a South London Population*, University of Reading and Kids Company, 2014

40 E Dowler, 'Budgeting for food on a low income in the UK: the case of lone-parent families', 22(5), 1997, pp405–17; E Dowler, S Turner and B Dobson, *Poverty Bites: food, health and poor families,* Child Poverty Action Group, 2001; JH McKendrick, S Cunningham-Burley and K Backett-Milburn, *Life in Low Income Families in Scotland: research report,* Scottish Executive Social Research, 2003; S Hall, S Knibbs, K Medien and G Davis, *Child Hunger in London: understanding food poverty in the capital*, Greater London Authority and Ipsos MORI Social Research Institute, 2013

41 T Ridge, *Childhood Poverty and Social Exclusion: from a child's perspective,* Policy Press, 2002; JH McKendrick, S Cunningham-Burley and K Backett-Milburn, *Life in Low Income Families in Scotland: research report,* Scottish Executive Social Research, 2003

42 O Gill and N Sharma, *Food Poverty in the School Holidays*, Barnardos South West, 2004; H Lambie-Mumford and L Sims, 'Charitable breakfast clubs and holiday hunger projects in the UK', in W Wills and R O'Connell (eds), *Children and Society*, Special issue: 'Children's and young people's food practices in contexts of poverty and inequality', 32(3), 2018, pp244–54

43 Alongside research on school staff perspectives on children and poverty (eg, National Education Union and Child Poverty Action Group, *Child Poverty and Education: a survey of the experiences of NEU members*, 2018), calls for more

emphasis on food provision for children during the school holidays have been driven by the All Party Parliamentary Groups on School Food and on Hunger in the UK. However, while the role of statutory provision and government funding have been discussed, to date the provision remains charitable and voluntary' (H Lambie-Mumford and L Sims, *Children's Experiences of Food and Poverty: the rise and implications of charitable breakfast clubs and holiday hunger projects in the UK*, Sheffield Political Economy Research Institute, SPERI British Political Economy Brief No.31, 2018, p247).

44 E Dowler and C Calvert, *Diets of Lone Parent Families: social policy research 71*, Joseph Rowntree Foundation, 1995; E Dowler and D O'Connor, 'Rights-based approaches to addressing food poverty and food insecurity in Ireland and UK', *Social Science and Medicine*, 74(1), 2012, pp44–51

45 E Dowler, 'Policy initiatives to address low-income households' nutritional needs in the UK', *Proceedings of the Nutrition Society*, 67(3), 2008, p289

46 T Ridge, *Childhood Poverty and Social Exclusion: from a child's perspective*, The Policy Press, 2002, p2

47 J Pike and D Colquhoun, 'The relationship between policy and place: the role of school meals in addressing health inequalities', *Health Sociology Review*, 18 (1), 2009, pp51–2

48 H Dimbleby and J Vincent, *The School Food Plan*, Department for Education, 2013, at www.schoolfoodplan.com/library; Department for Education press release, 'Free school lunch for every child in infant school', 17 September 2013, available at www.gov.uk/government/news/free-school-lunch-for-every-child-in-infant-school

49 In England, the qualifying benefits are: income support; income-based job-seeker's allowance; income-related employment and support allowance; support under Part VI of the Immigration and Asylum Act 1999; the guaranteed element of pension credit; child tax credit (provided there is not also an entitle-ment to working tax credit and the annual gross income is no more than £16,190); working tax credit run-on (paid for four weeks after the recipient stops qualifying for working tax credit); universal credit – for those applying on or after 1 April 2018, the household income must be less than £7,400 a year (after tax and not including any benefits).

50 S Royston, L Rodrigues and D Hounsell, *Fair and Square: a policy report on the future of free school meals,* The Children's Society, 2012

51 S Compton, 'Changes to free school meals will hurt struggling families', The Children's Society blog, 23 February 2018, at www.childrenssociety.org.uk/news-and-blogs/our-blog/changes-to-free-school-meals-will-hurt-struggling-families

52 R Farthing, *Going Hungry? Young people's experiences of free school meals*, Child Poverty Action Group and British Youth Council, 2012; S Royston, L Rodrigues and D Hounsell, *Fair and Square: a policy report on the future of free*

school meals, The Children's Society, 2012

53 R Farthing, *Going Hungry? Young people's experiences of free school meals*, Child Poverty Action Group and British Youth Council, 2012

54 See note 53, p28

55 M Nelson and others, *Schools Meals in Secondary Schools in England*, DfES Research Report RR557, Food Standards Agency/Department for Education and Skills, 2004

56 F Brooks, *The Link between Pupil Health and Wellbeing and Attainment,* Public Health England, 2014; Jamie Oliver Food Foundation, *A Report on the Food Education Learning Landscape*, 2017

57 All maintained schools in England, as well as academies and free schools set up before September 2010 or after June 2014, are legally required to meet the School Food Standards. Academies created between September 2010 and June 2014 are also encouraged to use them. However, only a minority have signed up to do so while recent research suggests patchy implementation associated with a lack of statutory monitoring (Jamie Oliver Food Foundation, 2017).

58 CS Hart, 'The School Food Plan and the social context of food in schools', *Cambridge Journal of Education*, 46(2), 2016, pp211–31

59 J Brannen and P Storey, 'Children's food practices at secondary school: the discourse of choice', *Health Education Research*, 13(1), 1998, pp73–86; J Pike, 'Foucault, space and primary school dining rooms', *Children's Geographies*, 6(4), 2008, pp413–22; CS Hart, 'The School Food Plan and the social context of food in schools', *Cambridge Journal of Education*, 46(2), 2016, pp211–31; W Wills, G Danesi, A Kapetanaki and L Hamilton, 2018 'The socio-economic boundaries shaping young people's lunchtime food practices on a school day', *Children and Society*, 32(3), 2018, p195–206

Three
Understanding food poverty

Dimensions of food poverty

Concepts of poverty and food poverty have a long history.[1] In this book, we draw principally on the multi-dimensional definition of poverty, developed by Peter Townsend in the 1950s and 1960s in Britain, in terms of relative deprivation experienced by children and households. We define food poverty as encompassing social as well as material deprivation.[2]

Central to concepts of poverty and food poverty is 'the notion of food scarcity or deprivation in the basic need for food'.[3] For example, Seebohm Rowntree's 1901 definition of poverty – based on the minimum income that people might expect to receive and below which no one could be expected to fall – included at its heart adequate food for 'physical efficiency'.[4] However, as Townsend argued, and Rowntree acknowledged,[5] no one could really be expected to live on this 'primary poverty income' in real life: '[s]ocial pressures, to drink in the local pub, to buy presents for the children, to be a normal social being especially in adversity, required a higher budget'.[6] People have social as well as physical needs; these cannot be usefully divided, since the ways in which seemingly 'basic' needs (for example, for nutrition) are met are social.[7] While a cup of tea, for instance, is not nutritionally important, offering tea to visitors makes 'a small contribution [...] towards maintaining the threads of social relationships'.[8]

Today, these 'social' dimensions of food and eating are widely included as part of consensually determined minimum socially acceptable standards of living that are about more than just physical survival.[9] The Joseph Rowntree Foundation's Minimum Income Standard (MIS), for example, takes account not only of the cost of spending that is essential for health but also describes what is needed for social inclusion.[10] The Food Budget Standard is calculated as part of MIS. This is the amount deemed necessary for a realistic, nutritious, socially acceptable diet for different types of families that allows for participation in customary activities, including additional amounts for seasonal events such as Christmas, other feast days and birthdays, and modest and occasional eating out.[11] Costed at Tesco, it includes the cost of food (and some alcoholic beverages) consumed inside and outside of the home. The Food Budget Standard sets out what is needed by children in four age groups – from birth to 18 years – recognising that children have different dietary and nutritional requirements at different ages. In this book, we have compared the families' reported expenditure with the Food Budget Standard, averaged across children's age groups. It is acknowledged that the ways in which people meet their food needs vary widely and there may be reasons other than economic ones that explain why households spend less than is publically determined as socially acceptable on food. An advantage of the qualitative research on which the book is based is that we are able to explore the reasons that families may be spending less – or more – than the Food Budget Standard.

Both the MIS research and the UK Poverty and Social Exclusion Study report an 'austerity effect' on families' social participation in relation to food. This means that while families still see the value in social activities such as eating out or entertaining family, friends and children's friends, they cannot afford them.[12] Nevertheless, eating outside of the home remains a norm in the sense that it is 'widely encouraged'[13] and something most people expect to be able to do from time to time.

Childhood and eating are 'deeply steeped in the consumer culture of our time'.[14] Children and teenagers are key targets of the food industry and advertisements for food and drink. As consumers, they are influenced by markets and by peers; 'far from being a result of individualized behaviour', being in a group requires young people to take into account what their peers 'choose' to eat'.[15] Evidence suggests that being able to eat out occasionally is a norm for the majority of young people, but that income plays a part in whether they are able to participate. Analysis of combined waves (2008/09–2013/14) of the National Diet and Nutrition Survey finds that around 70 per cent of young people aged 11–16 years ate out at least once or twice a month.[16] However, this is not evenly distributed: among the lowest two income deciles, the proportion who reported rarely or never eating a meal out is almost three times higher (41.5 per cent and 43.8 per cent in deciles 1 and 2 respectively) in comparison to the top two deciles (15.2 per cent and 15.2 per cent in 9 and 10 respectively).

While sociological studies of consumption have often emphasised its role in hierarchies of 'distinction',[17] sociologists of childhood note how children, particularly in low-income families, often look to consumer culture to establish a sense of belonging.[18] The costs of inclusion in childhood norms and customs may be too high for low-income families, but so too are the costs of exclusion in terms of being unable to 'fit in' and 'join in'.[19]

Understanding children's lives

There is a danger that food poverty measures and interventions abstract children from their families and wider circumstances that are so important for shaping and understanding their experiences.[20] In this book, we examine the everyday practices and perspectives of children as well as their parents. As sociologists of food, families and childhood, we view children as agents in their own lives at the same time as acknowledging that, as minors, they are financially dependent on, and legally the responsibility of, their parents. While children have some control over what they eat, their consumption of food and other goods cannot be understood in isolation or as independent of their family circumstances. Reflecting feminist and sociological work from the 1980s,[21] we also view the household as a resource system. We are interested in intra-household distribution; how resources are shared and managed between family members, including between parents and children.

In seeking to understand children's food practices in low-income families, we adopt an approach close to an 'ethnographic tradition' used in British community studies. By this, we do not mean that the study was based on observation; family studies conducted in people's homes typically preclude such methods. Rather, our approach is materialist in its focus on the mundane practices related to eating and food consumption. The concept of 'practices'[22] seeks to understand the habitual aspects of human behaviour that are not easily open to reflexive engagement and is well suited to the study of food. Focusing on the 'normal' aspects of everyday life is also a lens on what is 'non-normal' in the sense that it illuminates what young people regard as normative among their peers. This approach also helped us to meet our ethical obligations to children and young people in that our use of a 'practice approach' sought to avoid direct questions about poverty and disadvantage that might cause children embarrassment and shame. Questions about hunger were part of a self-completion questionnaire given to children to complete, in addition to the interview that included a number of standardised questions. The parents' interviews were supplemented by written 'checklists' of 'food coping strategies'.

Mothers and poverty

Seebohm Rowntree's 1901 measures of poverty failed to recognise the key part that mothers play in combating poverty through the management of household resources. In 1913, a study by Maud Pember Reeves was conducted in Lambeth and immortalised in her book, *Round about a Pound a Week*. The study was a milestone in the history of poverty in Britain and demonstrated the ways in which mothers with different numbers of children managed to get by. It is, however, salutary to note that the families Pember Reeves studied had an employed male provider and were not the poorest families, though among them were those whose jobs were precarious:[23]

> The lives of the children of the poor are shortened, and the bodies of the children of the poor are stunted and starved on a low wage. And to the insufficiency of a low wage is added the horror that it is never secure.

In the 1930s, the work of the Women's Health Enquiry Committee was seminal in redressing the lack of attention paid to the diet, health and conditions of poor working class women. It surveyed 1,250 housewives from across the country about budgets, menus and the strategies by which they managed. A striking finding concerned the ways in which 'the woman will starve herself in order that the children will have a little more'.[24]

A wealth of more recent research evidence describes how mothers living on low incomes 'get by'.[25] A consistent finding is that women are primarily responsible for managing money when there isn't enough and often go without food and other things to prioritise the needs of children and male partners – a strategy referred to as 'maternal sacrifice'[26] or 'maternal altruism'.[27] While anthropological research suggests such altruism it is not universal,[28] parenthood – and motherhood in particular – is often understood as a condition that should and does 'engender selflessness'.[29] As the social anthropologist Pat Caplan notes, the expectation that mothers sacrifice their food intake for others is one that many 'women have internalized to the point where it becomes second nature, and they may even articulate a preference for less valued food'.[30] Different entitlements to food are embedded in, and reproduce, relations of power, including those that are gendered.[31] The finding that women are both expected to, and do, practice maternal altruism towards both their children and their male partners, denying themselves food if there is not enough to go round, is reported in a number of sociological studies.[32]

Shame, reputation and stigma

Poverty is not only about material and social living conditions but also the active part that people living in poverty play in relation to those conditions. Some concepts focus on the ways in which those in poverty survive and resist the indignities of being designated 'poor'.[33] This approach has been heavily criticised for reducing poverty to cultural patterns of living. By contrast, Sen's approach tackles this by situating poverty at the intersection between the deprivation of individual capacities and the absence of opportunities, such as those of the labour market and the state.[34] Accordingly, the poverty line needs to be set at a level at which people can 'achieve adequate participation in communal activities and be free from public shame from failure to satisfy conventions'.[35]

This is Dayo and Ayo's mother's only cupboard in a shared kitchen. It contains oil, salt and some spices. She cannot always use the kitchen as the other residents complain that she has not paid towards the gas. She enjoys cooking and volunteers in the kitchen of a local charity but prefers to be given canned food by a charity that she can microwave in their room: '...you know, sometimes I don't like [the charity] giving me fresh food because of the people in when I want to cook; they start grumbling – "You don't pay for light, let us cook this this this..." But sometimes I just beg them to let me cook for the family.'

When food and housing are under threat, this can instill feelings of insecurity and a fear of the future.[36] Shame is commonly associated with a sense of insecurity and is seminal to understanding the experience of poverty. Some sociologists understand shame as being intrinsic to structures of power and prestige, while others pay attention to the way shame, as an emotion, drives people to maintain a positive self-image. The distinction between the externalisation of shame or shaming and the internal experience of feeling shame or shamed is useful. 'External shame' concerns how others, notably the media, wider kin, schools and many other institutions, view those in poverty. A deliberate consequence of austerity policies in Britain has been to intensify the stigmatisation of those living in poverty.[37] External shame generates and reinforces feelings of internal or 'personal shame' whereby individuals feel a sense of failure in not being valued by other people and not living up to their own expectations.[38] In individualist cultures, like Britain's, the experience of shame generally affects the person who transgresses social norms, as contrasted with collectivist societies where the shame attached to, and experienced by, individuals can cast a shadow over all members of the social group to which they belong.

> '…you never thought that you'd have to go through something like that, to be able to ask someone else for food for your children.' (mother of 12-year-old Troy)

Concepts of external and internal shame resonate with concepts of public and personal reputation.[39] Public reputation refers to the reputation of a group as a whole, a family for example, that is accountable to and sanctioned by external audiences. A personal reputation refers to a particular identity, as in the case of the 'good mother' who is accountable to members of her family, although personal reputation may become a matter of public reputation, where failure to care adequately for a child is brought to the attention of external authorities or public agencies and an individual is labelled and relegated to the rank of 'inadequate mother'.

As Chapter 5 demonstrates, mothers go to great lengths to protect their children from going without food and, in many cases, from the knowledge that they are struggling financially.

> 'Last week I didn't even eat for four days…And…I have to lie to my kids and tell them I've eaten so that they're okay, because as long as my kids are eating then I'm okay.' (mother of Shaniya, inner London)

Yet when family budgets are heavily constrained, mothers' efforts may not succeed in protecting their children and this affects children's lives and wellbeing. Moreover, many children were aware of their families' situations and some went without food.

Stigma is also experienced by children and 'the impact can be particularly devastating for a child or young person who is developing a sense of her own identity'.[40] The financial constraints that low-income families are under affect children's relations with their peers with whom they typically engage in processes of 'social comparison'.[41] Poverty can make children feel different from their friends when they are unable to take part in routine expected activities with them. As Chapter 7 shows, some children were unable to offer hospitality to friends at home – invitations to stay for tea or offers of a drink or snack – or they lacked spending money when they were out with their friends.

> 'If I had my own place, my own room, I could say 'yeah come over' but my mum [inaudible] I don't have a room, I'm just sharing with my mum. Then we haven't much food so…' (Amara, age 15, lives in a hostel in the inner London borough)

For many children, participation in activities outside the home, especially those involving food, were social norms and central to feelings of social inclusion. Where it was compromised, this often led to internal feelings of shame. In such situations, personal reputation was impugned, affecting children's social status in their peer groups that in turn had consequences for how children *felt* about their situations, in comparing themselves with others, and lowered their self-esteem.

Notes

1   S Maxwell, 'Food Security: a post-modern perspective', *Food Policy*, 21(2), pp155–70, 1996; E Dowler, M Kneafsey, H Lambie, A Inman and R Collier, 'Thinking about 'food security': engaging with UK consumers', *Critical Public Health*, 21, 2011, (4), p403–16; M Kneafsey, E Dowler, H Lambie, A Inman and R Collier, 'Consumers and food security: uncertain or empowered?' *Journal of Rural Studies*, 29, 2012, pp1–12

2   R O'Connell, C Owen, M Padley, A Simon and J Brannen, 'Which types of family are at risk of food Poverty in the UK? A relative deprivation approach', *Social Policy and Society*, 5 February 2018, 1–18, doi:10.1017/S1474746418000015

3   V Tarasuk, *Discussion Paper on Household and Individual Food Insecurity*, Health Canada, 2001, p7

4   BS Rowntree, *Poverty: a study of town life*, Macmillan, 1901

5   Rowntree later explained that the line was drawn at a lower level for political reasons to avoid being accused of 'crying for the moon': A Briggs, 'Seebohm Rowntree's Poverty: A Study of Town Life in historical perspective', in J Bradshaw and R Sainsbury (eds), *Getting the Measure of Poverty: the early legacy of Seebohm Rowntree*, Ashgate, 2000, p10

6   H Glennerster, J Hills, D Piachaud and J Webb, *One Hundred Years of Poverty and Policy*, Joseph Rowntree Foundation, 2004, p25

7   R Hick, 'Poverty as capability deprivation: conceptualising and measuring poverty in contemporary Europe', *European Journal of Sociology*, 55(3), 2014, p301

8   P Townsend, *Poverty in the United Kingdom: a survey of household resources and standards of living*, Allen Lane and Penguin Books, 1979, p50

9   A Davis, D Hirsch, N Smith, J Beckhelling and M Padley, *A Minimum Income Standard for the UK in 2012: keeping up in hard times,* Joseph Rowntree Foundation, 2012

10 N Oldfield and S Burr, *Minimum Income Standard: the food budget standard*, 2008, at http://www.lboro.ac.uk/media/wwwlboroacuk/content/crsp/downloads/MIS_thefoodbudgetstandard_workingpaper.pdf

11 A Davis, D Hirsch and M Padley, *A Minimum Income Standard for the UK in 2014,* Joseph Rowntree Foundation, 2014; M Padley and others, *A Minimum Income Standard for London 2016/17,* Trust for London, 2017

12 A Davis and others, *A Minimum Income Standard for the UK in 2012: keeping up in hard times,* Joseph Rowntree Foundation, 2012; J Gordon and others, *The Impoverishment of the UK: poverty and social exclusion UK first results: living standards,* Open University, 2013

13 P Townsend, *Poverty in the United Kingdom: a survey of household resources and standards of living,* Allen Lane and Penguin Books, 1979, p31

14 T Ridge, *Childhood Poverty and Social Exclusion: from a child's perspective,* Policy Press, 2002, p37

15 WJ Wills, K Backett-Milburn, S Gregory and J Lawton, 'The influence of the secondary school setting on the food practices of young teenagers from disadvantaged backgrounds in Scotland', *Health Education Research*, 20(4), 2005, p464

16 L Hamilton, *Young People's Food and Eating Practices: a comparison of higher and lower income households in a London Borough*, PhD thesis, University College London, forthcoming 2019

17 P Bourdieu, *Distinction: a social critique of the judgement of taste*, Harvard University Press, 1984

18 AJ Pugh, *Longing and Belonging: parents, children and consumer culture*, University of California Press, 2009

19 T Ridge, *Childhood Poverty and Social Exclusion: from a child's perspective,*

Policy Press, 2002; and see Chapter 4

20 H Lambie-Mumford and L Sims, '"Feeding Hungry Children": the growth of charitable breakfast clubs and holiday hunger projects in the UK', in W Wills and R O'Connell (eds), *Children and Society*, Special issue: 'Children's and young people's food practices in contexts of poverty and inequality', 32(3), 2018, pp244–54

21 For example: J Brannen and G Wilson (eds), *Give and Take in Families: studies in resource distribution*, Unwin Hyman, 1987; S Wallman, *Eight London Households*, Tavistock, 1984

22 Developed by A Reckwitz, 'Towards a theory of social practice: a development of cultural theorising', *European Journal of Social Theory*, 5(2), 2002, pp243–63 and E Shove, M Panzar and M Watson, *The Dynamics of Social Practice: the everyday and how it changes*, Sage, 2012

23 M Pember Reeves, *Round About a Pound a Week,* Persephone Books, 1913, p210

24 M Spring Rice, *Working-Class Wives: their health and conditions,* Virago, 1981 (first published by Penguin Books/Pelican Books in 1939), p157

25 R Lister, *Poverty,* Polity Press, 2004. The authors are aware of fewer studies that examine other forms of agency identified by Lister (getting out, getting back at and getting organised) in relation to families' food and eating practices. However, community food co-operatives and bulk buying schemes may be examples of the latter (eg, Gordon et al., 2018).

26 P Attree, 'Low-income mothers, nutrition and health: a systematic review of qualitative evidence', *Maternal and Child Nutrition* 1(4), 2005, pp227–40

27 A Whitehead, *I'm Hungry, Mum: the politics of domestic budgeting,* Routledge, 1984

28 N Scheper-Hughes, *Death Without Weeping: the violence of everyday life in Brazil,* University of California Press, 1992; H Land and H Rose call it 'compulsory altruism' in 'Compulsory altruism for some or an altruistic society for all?', in P Bean, J Ferris and D Whynes (eds), *In Defence of Welfare*, Tavistock, 1985

29 E Lewin, *Gay Fatherhood: narratives of family and citizenship in America,* University of Chicago Press, 2009, p129

30 P Caplan, 'Why do people eat what they do? Approaches to food and diet from a social science perspective', *Clinical Child Psychology and Psychiatry* 1(2), 1996, p218

31 A Sen, *Poverty and Famines: an essay on entitlement and deprivation*, Oxford University Press, 1981

32 For example: N Charles and M Kerr, *Women, Food and Families*, Manchester University Press, 1988; A Murcott, 'The cultural significance of food and eating', *Proceedings of the Nutrition Society*, 42(2), 1982, pp203–10; ML DeVault,

Feeding the Family: the social organization of caring as gendered work, University of Chicago Press, 1991; T Lobstein, 'Cheap or cheerful?', *Health Visitor*, 64(8), 1991; E Dowler and C Calvert, *Nutrition and Diet in Lone-parent Families in London*, Family Policy Studies Centre, 1995. Other strategies include 'strategic adjustment' to the 'discipline of poverty' (B Dobson and others, *Diet, Choice and Poverty: social, cultural and nutritional aspects of food consumption among low income families*, Family Policy Studies Centre, 1994) by those on persistently low incomes and 'resigned adjustment' that is characterised 'not only by economizing around shopping for food becoming a burden, but by the pleasure derived from eating also being diminished' (J Goode, 'Feeding the family when the wolf's at the door: the impact of over-indebtedness on contemporary foodways in low-income families in the UK', *Food and Foodways*, 20(1), 2012, p24).

33 For example, O Lewis, *The Children of Sanchez: autobiography of a Mexican family,* Vintage Books, 1961

34 A Sen, *Development as Freedom,* Oxford University Press, 1999

35 A Sen, 'Poor, Relatively Speaking', *Oxford Economic Papers*, 35(2), 1983, p167

36 R Walker, *The Shame of Poverty*, Oxford University Press, 2014

37 E Dowler, 'Food banks and food justice in "Austerity Britain"', in G Riches and T Silvasti (eds), *First World Hunger Revisited: food charity or the right to food?*, Palgrave Macmillan, 2014

38 See note 36

39 J Finch, *Family Obligations and Social Change*, Blackwell, 1989, pp188–92

40 R Lister, *Poverty*, Polity Press, 2004

41 L Festinger, 'A theory of social comparison processes', *Human Relations,* 7(2), 1954, pp117–40

Four

The *Families and Food in Hard Times* study

The 'Families and Food in Hard Times' study is funded by the European Research Council.[1] It examines the extent and experience of food poverty among children and families in three European countries: Portugal, Norway and the UK. Alongside secondary analysis of large-scale data, in all three countries qualitative interviews were carried out with young people aged 11–15 years,[2] and their parents or carers. Forty-five families took part in both the UK and Portugal and 43 families in Norway.

The aim of the study was to situate the families and children in particular communities in order to understand better their specific experiences and the conditions in which they live. Such a 'case study' approach sets out to examine families in situ, the particularities of each family, and to extrapolate from each family to other similar cases. The study was carried out in two contrasting study areas in each country, in the years 2015–2017. In the UK, 30 of the sample lived in an inner London borough and 15 in a coastal town in South East England, both areas with high child poverty rates of over 40 per cent (after housing costs).[3]

The local areas

The two UK study areas differ in terms of employment opportunities, housing costs and demographically, with the inner London borough being more ethnically mixed. Both are characterised by a high density of fast food outlets selling relatively cheap, energy-dense foods.[4] In the inner London borough, there is also a range of local and national supermarkets and shops as well as street markets, where fresh food is readily available. There is also a good public transport system, and buses for local children and young people are free. In the coastal area, by contrast, transport is expensive and there is a limited range of mainly low-budget food shops and outlets. Both areas are undergoing gentrification, though more recently in the coastal area, which became run down during the 1970s when British seaside resorts went out of fashion. The areas differ in their education systems, with implications for children mixing with those from different class and ethnic backgrounds. In the London borough, academies and community schools dominate and, in this diverse area, schools have a socio-economic mix.[5] In the coastal area, there is a grammar school system. As the most deprived families living in such areas only have a 6 per cent chance of attending a selective school,[6] the class intakes of the schools attended by most of the children in the coastal area were more homogenous.

The inner London borough: a densely populated urban area

The typical mix of housing in the inner London borough – local authority estate and Victorian terrace

Streets undergoing gentrification – a chicken shop and a trendy café in the inner London borough

Typical multiple occupancy housing in the coastal area

Run down seaside resort post-1970s

The coastal area

Methodology

Families in both areas were recruited via a short self-completion survey sent to parents of children in three schools. This was followed by other recruitment methods, such as referrals from local charities providing help to families and persons in need. Careful attention was given to ensuring ethical standards were adhered to throughout the study. For example, obtaining informed consent was seen as an ongoing process: parents were asked for their own consent and for permission to seek the child's consent to participate, prior to carrying out the interview. In most cases, interviews took place in the home; some parents chose to be interviewed elsewhere, such as at a trusted organisation or in a public place. Leaflets explaining the study were provided to parents and young people prior to the interviews. Both parents and young people were asked for their consent again before the interviews began. Anonymity and confidentiality were assured, with the exception of any safeguarding concerns being raised. Pseudonyms are used in the case studies to protect the anonymity of participants.

The aim of the study was to gain insight into these families in as much depth as possible, given the limits of our resources. Semi-structured interviews were conducted with parents (usually mothers, but included a lone father, lone grandmother and male partners in four of the couple families) and young people (30 boys and 21 girls). Interviews included the topics of income and outgoings, food budgets and practices, social lives regarding food and eating, sources of support and perspectives on managing and feeding the family on a low income. While we sought to interview parents and children separately, housing conditions meant this was not always possible. Interviews with parents lasted roughly 1.5 hours and with young people around 45 minutes. A subsample of families (12/45) participated in two follow-up visits that involved visual methods, to learn more about foods bought and eaten at home and elsewhere and how any changes in circumstances impacted on food and eating over time.[7] These visual methods included a tour and photography of the family's kitchen and food storage areas with the parent, followed by an interview with the young person about the photos s/he had taken of food s/he had eaten recently in different settings, such as home, at friend's places and out in the neighbourhood. A selection of the photographs are used throughout the book – while some are not of usual print quality, we feel it is important to include them. In most cases, and with parents' and young people's permission, interviews were recorded and transcribed verbatim.

A key challenge in the methodology was recruitment of the sample. As poverty is imbued with stigma and prejudice, research which seeks to explore its impact needs to be conducted with great sensitivity, especially when it involves children and young people.[8] Given the focus of the research, the purposive nature of the sample and what we were asking of families in terms of their time and personal experiences, recruitment and completion of interviews required a great deal of time and effort over a two-year period. Another challenge was that while we sought to interview children and parents separately, housing conditions did not always permit this. In some cases, the timing of interviews also demonstrated the dynamic nature of poverty. For example, one mother was interviewed a few weeks before her child. In the intervening period the mother lost her job and visited a food bank. While the mother did not report a lack of food at the first visit, her child reported it at the second (see Chapter 5).

The analysis of the information gathered involved treating the families as 'whole cases' – to view all the material from one family together and setting them in the societal context of social inequality. Our aim was also to take account of the intersecting characteristics of each household, for example, the type of household, the ethnic backgrounds of family members, parents' employment status and family size. We also wrote extensive field notes about the neighbourhoods, the settings in which the interviews were conducted and the encounters between the interviewees and interviewer, material that was an important part of the analysis. Together the research team rigorously and systematically compared the cases, analysing the commonalities and differences between them.[9] Children's responses and enthusiasm for talking about the place of food in their lives varied considerably, which is unsurprising given the range of ages, personalities and backgrounds. Further, food is not always a topic that is easy to reflect or elaborate upon. The admission of lack of food is moreover highly problematic and may provoke admission of failure, stigma or feelings of shame. Thus, the broken or truncated speech in which many children responded is open to interpretation.

The families

The sample reflects the diversity of family forms, although a disproportionate number (30/45) – ie, two-thirds – are lone-parent families (Appendix 1, Table 1.1). It includes households in which one or more parents are in work and those who are on benefits. Lone parents (mothers) were often in paid work although, as many studies of those on low incomes show, poverty is not necessarily a stable condition. People move in and out of employment; benefit regimes and entitlements change; and people's lives are beset by other kinds of life events. Some of the most deprived children in the study were children in families whose legal status in Britain was problematic[10] and, as a result, they had 'no recourse to public funds'. These families are not typical of those living in poverty in the UK. However, destitute migrant families are invisible in large-scale survey research, while their experiences reflect the devastating effects of successive governments' regulation of welfare benefits as a tool for controlling immigration.[11]

More than half of the sample (25/45) had at least one adult in paid work, while four families had no formal source of income at all (Appendix 1, Table 1.2). Comparing the income of our families to the pattern of household income nationally,[12] most were in the bottom two of five income groups: 21/45 were in the lowest fifth and 20/45 were in the second lowest fifth. A few families (4/45) families were in the middle income group. In the lowest income group, about as many families had at least one adult in paid work (9/21) as were reliant on benefits (8/21), while in the second lowest income group, around twice as many families had at least one adult in paid work (13/45) as were reliant only on benefits (7/45) (Appendix 1, Table 1.2). Those (4/45) with neither pay nor benefits were concentrated at the bottom in the lowest group. Thirty-nine of the families were in debt,

Shola's evening meal: 'One's okra and red stew, the other one's eba.' She explained: 'You don't use gas to make it, you only use hot water [...] It has no flavour, so you can't really eat it by itself. So it's, like, just...basically you're, like, eating paper...like that, so you have to have something with it, which gives it the flavour.'

which included credit cards, loans, rent or utility arrears and high-interest rent-to-own purchases.

In both areas, around half the mothers were British but in the coastal area all the British mothers (8/15) were white. In the inner London borough, there was more diversity among the British mothers (18/30) that included white British and black British as well as British Asian mothers, while a third (10/30) of mothers had migrated from outside the European Union (West and North Africa). In the total sample, parents in 7/45 families were migrants from mainland Europe (Appendix 1, Table 1.3) and the majority of these (5/7) lived in the coastal area. In the former group, there were several cases in which the parents and children had been cut off from state benefits while the families were in the (lengthy) legal process of applying for 'leave to remain'.

Just over half (23/45) of parents were experiencing the most severe dimensions of food poverty. They reported eating an inadequate quantity of food and experiencing hunger, skipping meals and using food banks, for example. In about a quarter of the cases (12/45), the quantity of food children were eating was also compromised, meaning they also went hungry at times.

Two-thirds (37/45) of the families, including those reporting hunger, were affected by living on a low income in other ways with regard to food and eating. These included having to limit the quality and range of foods purchased and cooked (quality), not being able to participate socially by eating with family and friends at home or outside (social participation), and worrying about whether food would run out before having money to buy more (worry). Around a fifth of families (8/45) did not experience these dimensions of food poverty but did report that food budgets were 'constrained' such that they sometimes had to spend less on food to be able afford other things. This did not, however, involve compromising food quantity, quality (nutritional) or social participation (Table 4.1).[13]

Table 4.1

Dimensions of food poverty experienced by adults and children

	Food quantity	Any of: quality, social participation, worry	Food budget constrained only	None
Adult	23	37	8	0
Child	13	31	n/a	14

Notes

1 The research has received funding from the European Research Council under the European Union's Seventh Framework Programme (FP7/2007–2013)/ERC grant agreement number 337977.

2 There were three outliers: one 10-year-old and two who were 16 either at the first or second interview.

3 See the interactive maps and statistics at www.endchildpoverty.org.uk.

4 E Maguire, T Burgoine and P Monsivais, 'Area deprivation and the food environment over time: a repeated cross-sectional study on takeaway outlet density and supermarket presence in Norfolk, UK, 1990–2008', *Health and Place*, 33, 2015, pp142–47

5 D Dorling, 'Viewpoint: Britain is a segregated society – the isolation of the richest from the rest', *Discover Society*, May 2018

6 S Burgess, C Crawford and L Macmillan, 'Grammar schools: why academic selection only benefits the very affluent', *The Conversation*, 8 March 2017, at https://theconversation.com/grammar-schools-why-academic-selection-only-benefits-the-very-affluent-74189

7 R O'Connell, 'The use of visual methods with children in a mixed methods study of family food practices', *International Journal of Social Research Methodology*, 16(1), 2013, pp31–46

8 T Ridge, *Childhood Poverty and Social Exclusion: from a child's perspective*, Policy Press, 2002, p9

8 R Gomm, M Hammersley and P Foster, 'Case study and generalisation', in R Gomm, M Hammersley and P Foster (eds), *Case Study Method*, Sage, 2000

10 They did not have the immigration status of 'indefinite leave to remain'.

11 R O'Connell and J Brannen, 'Food poverty and the families the state has turned its back on: the case of the UK', in HP Gaisbauer, G Schweiger and C Sedmak (eds), *Absolute Poverty in Europe: interdisciplinary perspectives on a hidden phenomenon*, Policy Press, 2019

12 Taking into account household size and calculated after housing costs. See Appendix 2 for details.

13 See A Nielsen and L Holm, 'Making the most of less', *Food, Culture and Society*, 19(1), 2016, pp71–91

Five

Going without and getting by

This chapter looks at the everyday realities of food poverty for children and parents in Britain today. It examines some of the conditions in which children and families are unable to access enough food or the types of food that make for a nutritious diet, the ways they manage and how it makes them feel.

Having enough to eat of adequate quantity and quality has long been a minimal expectation of what it means to live in a western country. Our study, however, found families who were unable to feed themselves properly and some who were barely able to do so. In some families, parents often went without food to prevent their children being hungry, while, in others, both parent and child suffered.

More than half of the parents in our study went without enough to eat at times. They said they ate less than they needed and skipped meals, while some used food banks. Despite parents' sacrifices, young people in over a quarter of families also went hungry (Table 5.1).

Table 5.1 shows the four groups we divided the families into.

Table 5.1

Parents going without food by child reports of going hungry (N=45)

		Child feels hungry		
		YES	NO	
Parent goes without	YES	A. Parent and child go without and are hungry (11 cases)	B. Parental sacrifice means child gets enough to eat (12 cases)	23
	NO	C. Parent gets enough to eat but child does not (1 case)	D. Neither parent nor child goes without enough food or is hungry (21 cases)	22
		12	33	45

A. Parent and child both go without enough food and are hungry; some of these families are literally 'destitute', by any definition of the term.

B. Parent goes without and is hungry but child gets enough to eat.

C. Parent gets enough food but child does not (a pattern related to the fluctuating nature of (food) poverty and the different times in which the parent and child were interviewed).

D. Neither parent nor child goes without enough food or is hungry.

Below we look at each group and examine children's everyday food experiences.

Group A: parents and children go without enough food and are hungry

In around a quarter of the families, children went hungry despite parents sacrificing food to try to protect them. All families, except one, in this group were headed by lone mothers. Nearly all these families were in the lowest income group (see Appendix 1, Table 1.2), reflecting that, in most cases, they were not in formal paid employment. Four of the seven mothers were migrants who were neither allowed to work nor to claim benefits because their immigration status meant they have no recourse to public funds. These four families were dependent on charity and were in 'absolute' poverty.[1]

Charlie and Amara both regularly go hungry though, as their case studies show, their circumstances and experiences are very different.

Charlie

Charlie (age 15, white British) lives with his mother, a lone parent, in the inner London borough. Charlie's mother lost her job as a teacher two years ago. She has a weekly income of £166 a week made up of job-seeker's allowance, child tax credit and child benefit. They live in social housing and the rent is covered by housing benefit. They are in the lowest income group and spend about £30 a week on food. This is around half of the Food Budget Standard for this type of family (see p19). Charlie's mother has used a food bank twice recently because of a large gas bill and bank overdraft charges. She no longer eats breakfast, regularly skips meals and buys lower quality food. She cannot afford to buy the fresh fish or cuts of meat that she used to buy and says she is *'skipping some really nice things that I used to really like'*. Charlie, she claims, eats a lot and – typical of teenagers – is always hungry. She is very concerned because her son is growing fast but also because he eats a lot of processed food. As a mother she feels she is letting him down.

Charlie says he is always hungry. He does not eat breakfast. At school, he uses his £2 free school meal (FSM) allocation at breaktime (Figure 5.1). By lunchtime, he is hungry again. If he has lunch at school, he is restricted to a small sandwich costing £1.80 because the cost of the larger baguette he would prefer exceeds his FSM allowance and, in any case, he has usually spent his allowance by then. So he goes home for lunch, typically pasta or noodles, but he claims *'sometimes there's no food'*.

Charlie's mother said: 'I like to have a full fridge, cupboards… it's depressing having an empty cupboard. It's horrible to open the fridge…and Charlie will open the fridge and go "What's in here?" like "Oh okay". I'm not really providing enough'.

Figure 5.1

Charlie's typical school day menu

Breakfast	No breakfast at home or school
Breaktime	Uses FSM allowance for a snack at break
Lunch	Goes home for lunch and makes something quick and easy (eg, instant noodles) if there is food (not always)
Evening meal	Prefers ready meals and sweet things
Snacks	Chips after school (£1); grazes; toast with chocolate spread; Weetabix with milk, if there is some, or dry if not

After school, he hunts for food at home again:

> 'I just see what's in the house, look in the fridge, look in the cupboard. Look in the fridge again, hoping more food's just appeared.'

In the evenings, his mother says she 'pads out' meals but, because Charlie does not like the pulses she uses, she ends up making two meals. She cooks him sausages, pizza, pasta or noodles. He claims that he eats *'pretty much the same thing'* every day. Asked how he would like it to be different he said:

> 'I don't know. Just like more fresh food like, not just frozen food all the time like. Frozen food's nice, don't get me wrong, but sometimes it's nice for like a meal, like an actual meal like. Like a Sunday roast, like a meal like that... not just like one little pizza or like a burger.'

After dinner, Charlie feels hungry again and, after his mother has gone to bed, he eats more pasta or noodles, or a frozen burger. The foods he puts together often make for unconventional meals. Charlie reports that food is more plentiful when his mother's benefits are paid and she has been shopping at Iceland.

Charlie reported 'often' going to both school and to bed hungry. When there is insufficient food at home, he fantasises about a *'big meal'* while eating *'little bowls of pasta'* saying:

> '...even if I do get food it's not like a sufficient amount, so I'd still be hungry after I eat it. Especially as I've got a fast metabolism as well, I just like to eat.'

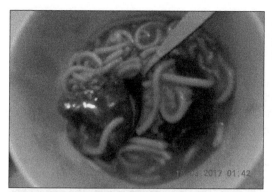

'There was only one burger left and spaghetti, so I just mixed it together.'

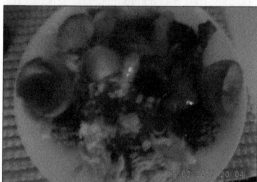

A roast dinner Charlie enjoyed at his friend's house. He said: 'It's got, like rice, chicken, gravy, Yorkshire pudding…stuffing, carrots, broccoli, potatoes.'

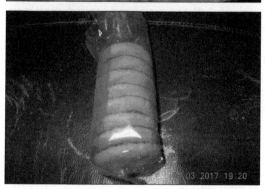

Charlie's mum bought Jaffa Cakes that he ate a pack and a half of: 'There's not usually that type of stuff in the house.'

Asked when gets hungry, he answered: *'I'm hungry right now'*. Unsurprisingly, Charlie has aspirations for becoming a chef: *'I just kind of like the idea of it, and I like the fact that you can just eat whenever you wanted…'*. Children's imagined futures are shaped in different ways by their current circumstances;[2] for Charlie, becoming a chef is a way of 'getting out'.[3]

Amara

Amara (age 15) lives in a hostel in inner London. She was born in southern Europe and lives with her mother, who is originally from North Africa. They recently moved to the UK, as her mother wanted *'to give my daughter education'*. After initially living with friends, they were placed in temporary accommodation in one room in a very large hostel but, when we interviewed them, they were facing eviction. Amara's mother is registered at the job centre and is seeking work. However, as she has no recourse to public funds, she cannot claim benefits. They rely on help from friends and sometimes the mother does informal, 'cash-in-hand' work.

There is no food budget. They live hand to mouth. The mother has used a food bank but, on the last occasion, was turned down because she had used up her quota of three visits a year. She protested unsuccessfully:

'I said sorry, well, we have to eat. Well, we're [not] eating just three times a year. I'm sorry to say that, I'm sorry. Well, we're eating every day, humans. She said, "this is how it work".'

Both Amara and her mother act in ways that suggest a great deal of sacrifice and altruism. Each considers the needs of the other and this extends to the limited quantity and quality of food. Amara's mother says: *'I say "well okay I can struggle, I can starve for my daughter", you understand, I want her to have proper education, proper stuff'*. She goes without food during the day and reserves what little there is for the evening when they eat together:

'Sometimes like I don't [eat] nothing just – I wait for my daughter to come at home and we have sandwich which we have, well, tin of tuna or something like that, you understand? I can starve all day long waiting for her, like, then we can share what we have at home. This is how it is, you understand?... morning I had coffee and that's it really, yeah, soft drinks or something or some toast. This is my day.'

Figure 5.2
Amara's typical school day menu

Breakfast	No breakfast at home or school
Lunch	Sometimes nothing; sometimes a sandwich
Evening meal	Sandwich; lasagne when can afford ingredients; pizza sometimes
Snacks	The interviewer felt unable to ask

Amara often goes to both school and bed hungry (Figure 5.2). Like her mother, she sacrifices her own food intake:

> 'I skip meals to share with my mum [inaudible]…for example, I skip my meal to wait for her to come back and at least we can have the same amount of food…[we] starve together through the whole day, so at least we will have had something to eat.'

When her mother has no money, Amara gives any she has to her mother. Ineligible for FSMs, Amara was not eating anything at school which affected her school work:

> 'I used to starve in school because…well I couldn't manage to make sandwiches at home or take crisps or whatever [inaudible] so I was just starving in school for the whole day.'

> 'When I'm hungry I just can't concentrate, it's really, really hard for me to do that…so I just need to make my mind up and know that I will eat after five hours, seven hours when I get home.'

Amara's mother eventually spoke to the school which now provides Amara with free lunches from discretionary funds. However, the £2 daily allowance does not go far as, for example, '*a small sandwich is like £1.60*'. Although Amara would like to take cheaper food from home, she says '*…when I don't have food at home what am I going to do?*' As Chapter 6 discusses, school meals can be vital for children living in poverty, but they are not always adequate.

Amara and her mother enjoy, and take a pride in, cooking. They cook Mediterranean dishes and are '*learning to cook English*'. They prefer fresh, home-cooked food. However, they find ingredients for cooking from scratch more expensive than ready-made meals. They eat much less meat and fish than they would like. Moreover, the reality of their lives leaves little scope for preparing homemade food. In their one room, they have poor cooking facilities and unhygienic conditions in which to store food (the building has cockroaches).

Group B: parents go without enough to eat but children are not directly affected by hunger

We now look at the group in which parents manage to protect their children from hunger by going without enough to eat themselves. Around half the parents who sacrificed their food intake were successful in protecting their children from going without food. Just over half of these were headed by lone parents (five mothers, one father and one grandmother) and the rest were couples. In the couple households, some mothers said they ate less than their partners, but two fathers in this group who were interviewed also reported eating less or differently from their children. In one family in which the mother said they ate less meat because of a lack of money, the father, who was reluctant to admit they are struggling, said this was a matter of preference.

All but one of these families were in the lowest two income groups (see Appendix 1, Table 1.2). In half of the families, at least one parent was in paid employment and, in half of these cases, income fluctuated because of variable or zero-hour contracts. In the other half of the parents, caring responsibilities, disability or ill health meant they were not employed. All but one of these families were in receipt of benefits.

Parental sacrifice is, in some cases, a response to fluctuating income or outgoings. Maddy's grandmother, for example, says she skips meals once or twice a week during the school holidays when Maddy is not getting FSMs. For Owen's family, an unexpected expense, combined with a variable income, means that at times there is less money for food. In other cases, where there is chronic low income, skipping meals and eating less is an established way that parents manage. Faith's father, a lone parent in full-time low-paid employment, skips food in the morning to ensure his four children can eat. Femi's mother does not eat at work, saving what money and food there is for her children.

Some parents internalise a preference for eating less or lower-valued foods – for example, Maya's mother claims she is 'not bothered' about going without fish or meat so her children can eat them. Some parents also seek to protect children from knowing that they are sacrificing their own food intake. Shaniya's mother says:

> '…last week I didn't even eat for four days. […] And […] I have to lie to my kids and tell them I've eaten so that they're okay, because as long as my kids are eating then I'm okay.'

However, some children worry and feel guilty about their parents' altruism. For example, Bryony (age 13) lives in a home in which food is often scarce. Her mother has faced many challenges, including what she describes as a 'poor' childhood and more recently psychological distress and related conditions as well as relationship breakdown. She depends on jobseeker's allowance, child tax credit and child benefit and says they are *'totally skint'*. Recently, when her *'benefits were stopped'*, they relied only on child benefit for the whole six-week summer holiday. Bryony says that:

> 'If there isn't enough food, we'll get it and sometimes mum will go hungry and starve and stuff. Even if it's not that much food for me and [brother], it's enough that we've actually had something, whereas mum hasn't, and it gets a bit to the point where we'll start feeling guilty because mum hasn't had anything and we've had it.'

Bryony's mother is creative at making meals out of very little. She said she was going to use the margarine along with flour in the cupboard to make pastry for a pie and 'I've got one of these… carrots…and then all I've got to do is go and buy meat'.

While parental sacrifice may protect children from the direct effects of food shortage, the indirect effects of poverty penetrate deeply into the 'emotional heartland' of children's personal and family lives.[4]

Bryony's mother's cupboard on the day before her benefits are paid. However, as she shops daily, there is usually 'not a lot' more food than this. 'There'll be a couple of tins of beans, tomatoes, basic things like that as a basis and then I've got my herbs and spices and stuff, and then I can just go out, buy meat and make something little.'

We now look at two case studies in this group. Both children live in two-parent families in the coastal area but their circumstances are otherwise different.

Emma

Emma (age 12, white British) is one of four children. Both of her parents are in poor health and neither is employed. The family is in the lowest income group (Appendix 1, Table 1.2). Their income comprises jobseeker's allowance, child tax credit and child benefit, as well as housing benefit to cover the rent. The parents' claims for employment and support allowance and personal independence payment were unsuccessful. Living in an isolated area with little transport, expensive bus fares and no free or subsidised travel for children, the family prioritises running a car that, along with debt repayments, squeezes their budget.

Emma's family relies on her grandparents' support, including food from their allotment: 'We get a lot of fresh veg in season. So, we've got marrow out there, fresh ones. We get carrots when it's time, we get all sorts of stuff...parsnips.'

Spaghetti bolognaise. Emma's mother said: 'A couple of times a week, when the money gets tight, we will end up with mince because…the amount of stuff we add to it, it makes it enough for two meals.'

The family spends about £90 to £100 a week on food. This is about two-thirds of the Food Budget Standard (see p19). The children all receive FSMs. The parents give the older two children £9 or £10 a week to top up their FSMs as the allowance *'isn't enough'*. They rely on the maternal grandparents' support to cover essential costs (such as dinner for the children) and emergencies (such as car repairs). They also depend on food the grandparents grow in their allotment.

The family's diet is of a mixed quality. Some meals are based on fresh ingredients, such as stuffed marrow and spaghetti bolognaise; others are cheap frozen foods, like pies and chips. When money is particularly tight, the quality and quantity of food suffers, as Emma's father says:

> 'You know, when you get a bigger bill come in, and that has to be paid – things like the electric and the others, then we find we're cutting down on the amount we buy, but then we're also cutting down on the quality.'

Both parents skip meals at times or miss out what they regard as 'protein' so that there is enough for the children. The mother says: *'we'll get the chips…but we won't get the sausage or the fish.'* The father adds: *'Yeah, they [the children] come first, and it's their money that we're getting it out of basically.'*

The children confirm that food shortages do not affect them directly. Emma says she never goes to school or bed hungry because of a lack of food. She is receiving treatment from a dietician for being underweight, but her father says this is as a result of her having very little interest in eating. Neither the parents nor the child connect this to the shortage of money and food at home. It is known however that children, particularly girls and young women, can internalise financial stress in different ways.[5]

Figure 5.3

Emma's typical school day menu

Breakfast	Cereal bar and Yakult at home – but often skips
Breaktime	Doughnut or sausage roll
Lunch	Chicken burger and drink (FSM)
Evening meal	Chicken nuggets and chips
Snacks	Crackers or bread and butter

Frozen gammon steaks with mash potato, frozen vegetables and gravy. Emma admits to being a 'fussy' eater but says: 'I eat anything pig.'

Prawn cocktail crisps. Her mother took this picture saying: 'She's supposed to have had them for breakfast this morning but she didn't pick them up.'

Generally, food does not interest Emma; she has to be reminded to eat and admits to being a 'fussy' eater. She does not always eat breakfast but, when she does, she has a cereal bar and yoghurt drink that the dietician recommended. She has FSMs. At breaktime, she says she has '*a sausage roll or something*' which costs 80p from the £2 the top-up her parents give her daily. With the rest of the money, '*sometimes I get some more food at lunch or I get a drink at lunch*'. She does not think her diet is particularly healthy but questions the messages given to her: '*The teachers that do it don't even believe in five a day.*' Her favourite food is KFC which she has '*once a month if I'm lucky*'.

Owen

Owen (age 12, white British) has one sibling. He has a mild learning disability and a bowel problem that requires regular medication, both of which affect what he eats. His parents are both in low-paid employment. As both parents work and there are only two children, the family is less squeezed financially than Emma's. His father works full time in a warehouse. His mother works part time, on a zero-hour contract, as a home carer and her pay is unpredictable. As the parents earn above the threshold for tax credits, there is no benefits safety net. Owen's mother's take-home pay varies between £800 and £1,100 a month, while she says her partner's is a '*solid £1,200*'. Owen's mother has to travel long distances in her job, but her work mileage allowance is insufficient and she partly meets the cost of petrol from the family's child benefit.

They spend around £125 a week on food and keeping costs down is the key priority. This is slightly over the Food Budget Standard (see p19), although Owen's special dietary requirements are catered for. The mother says she buys food that is filling rather than nutritious and that '*if cost was no bother…the kitchen would be completely full of fruit and veg. It really would.*'

As highlighted in Chapter 2, having an income that is low and unpredictable is stressful and affects food and eating. When money is very tight, Owen's mother says they purchase cheaper products:

'…on some days, well some months, when we can't afford it we'll go and get the pound for four [burgers]. Yeah, the really cheap, tacky things that are virtually full of fat. Yeah, we do things like that.'

They also eat food that goes further: '*It's usually spag bol, because that stretches. You can get a couple of days out of that.*' When there is little money for food:

> 'We usually run down the freezer…if it's looking rather really, really bare, then as long as the boys are fed then that's how it goes.'

The parents often go without proper meals while the children's food needs are prioritised. At the end of the month, and when there are additional costs – such as birthdays, Christmas and buying school uniforms – or unexpected expenses, such as a vet's bill, the parents skip lunch and resort to sandwiches or toast in the evenings:

> 'You know the reason we're on toast at the moment, like I say, is because of having the dog put down. That came straight out of his wages. We didn't even do, we couldn't even do, a shop.'

The mother says she goes '*past the hunger*' and dismisses this as something she and the children's father are content to do:

> 'So we cut back. As long as, like I say, as long as the kids are fed, we don't care about us. We'll sit, we're happy to just sit there and have toast every evening, so we do cut back a lot.'

Figure 5.4
Owen's typical school day menu

Breakfast	Chocolate Weetos at home
Lunch	Bacon panini, hot dog or sausage roll plus water
Evening meal	Spaghetti bolognaise, roast dinner, burger and chips, meatballs, frozen vegetables
Snacks	Crisps, grapes, doughnuts

Owen is not directly affected by shortages of food at home and eats three meals a day, plus snacks (Figure 5.4). He confirms that he never goes to school or bed hungry. However, he only likes a narrow range of foods. When asked what he thinks is a healthy diet, he suggests it comprises lots of fruit and vegetables but says his diet is '*not completely healthy*' because he eats '*a lot of bacon*'. Owen's parents try to cater to his tastes:

'We usually know what he likes. He likes his like jam doughnuts, we usually buy him a packet of jam doughnuts a week'. Because Owen is not entitled to FSMs, his mother gives him £1.50 a day for school lunch. She is concerned that this is not enough:

> 'I'm worried because I don't know how big the slice of pizza is or...because he's not...in my eyes, he's not eating a lot. He's a growing lad, he should be eating a lot more than that.'

While Owen's mother says he does not ask for more money, it is known that children moderate and manage their needs to avoid putting stress on their mothers.[6]

Group C: parent gets enough to eat but child does not

Given the moral and legal imperative for parents to protect their children, a child going hungry while the parent does not would ordinarily amount to 'neglect'. It is significant that only one of our families fell into this category and did so for a circumstantial reason, namely the significant gap in the timing of the interviews of parent and child. By the time the child was interviewed, her mother had stopped work and returned to college, with negative consequences for the family's current income and the food budget. So while the mother did not report going short of food at her interview, by the time her daughter was interviewed the situation had changed and they had visited a food bank. The case highlights how food poverty – and poverty in general – is often the result of marked fluctuations and uncertainty in income. It tells us something about the methodologies for researching poverty and the dynamic nature of poverty itself.

Group D: neither parent nor child goes without enough food or is hungry

Around half the families were 'getting by'; that is, they did *not* report an inadequate quantity of food, experiencing hunger, skipping meals or using food banks. In these families, the children do not report actually going without food, but this does not mean they are all well nourished.

To feed their families on little money, mothers describe a variety of ways they manage. Some parents, particularly first-generation migrants, have established ways of cooking in which they make dishes from fresh ingredients that are part of their cultural heritage. This typically involves large investments of time. Some mothers, mainly white British, have established ways of feeding the family that utilise pre-prepared and processed foods. All parents, whatever the origin of their cuisine, describe hunting for bargains, making dishes that are cheap and bulking out meals to make them 'stretch'.

Below, we briefly describe two cases that are emblematic of these different ways of managing. Both require considerable investments in terms of time. The third case we discuss is of a family in which the quality of food, particularly the amount of fruit and vegetables that the family can buy, is seriously compromised by low income.

Customary cooking practices

Anna (age 15, Eastern European) is one of four children in a two-parent family in the coastal area. They live in a privately rented flat. They are a Roma family and came to the UK seven years ago from the Czech Republic. Anna's father works 24 hours a week in a factory, where the mother also worked until she had her son, whom she now cares for full time. Their income from employment is supplemented with child tax credit and housing benefit. They spend around £100 a week on food for the family of six. This is around two-thirds of the Food Budget Standard (see p19).

Anna's mother finds food prices much cheaper in Britain than the Czech Republic and the quality much the same. Since arriving in the UK, they have not usually worried about affording food. However, a tax credits payment error left the family with a '*lot less*' money for food for two weeks following a change in the father's hours – although it was resolved and repaid quickly.

Anna's mother cooks meals based on Czech cuisine – stews and soups with vegetables, chicken, beef, rice, potatoes – that the family eats together at 'lunchtime', which is after school at around 4 o'clock. '*Like we don't eat the same food every day, every day we have different foods.*' Later in the evenings, the family has snacks or processed food like oven chips and frankfurters. The mother spends much of her time shopping for food and preparing meals. She buys in bulk where possible and shops at the cheapest shops but also finds some ingredients in the local Polish shops, which are more expensive. Anna's mother says she never throws food away.

Figure 5.5

Anna's typical school day menu

Breakfast	None
Lunch	Czech bread with salami or cheese, nuts or crisps, water (packed lunch)
Evening meal	Czech food like soup, rice and chicken, chips
Snacks	Chocolate, crisps, ice cream

Anna's tastes are rather different from that of her family. Anna is not keen on vegetables, unlike her siblings who enjoy them, but she likes fruit. She says that when she came to Britain she found it difficult to adapt to the British diet, especially school lunches which she claims have '*too many chips*'. She is now adapting to the 'local diet' practised by her friends, even though she says she still prefers Czech food. As a consequence, she considers her diet now to be '*less healthy*'. When asked about her favourite food, she mentions that she likes visiting the chip shop. Despite her mother's efforts to provide healthy food for the family, as is typically the case in migrant families, the mother is keen for her daughter to acculturate but also worries she is losing the taste for 'traditional' (Czech) food and preferring British food, which she views as less healthy.

Hunting for bargains

Many families say they manage by searching for reduced items and special offers, although for some, ill health and disability restrict this possibility. Cole (age 14, white British) lives in the coastal town with his parents and three younger siblings. His parents work in the care sector but are only able to work part-time because of the qualifying criteria of their working tax credit; if they exceed a certain number of hours they will be worse off.

Cole's mother feeds her large family by shopping around and looking for the best deals. In this family, the children contribute to managing food on a low income by helping with shopping. She says to the three children present:

'We don't have extravagant food, do we? Whenever we go shopping, we don't always buy the cheapest, like the shop's own brand of everything, but we do always look for the best deal, don't we? And you're very good at pointing them out for us, aren't you?'

Cole, as the eldest, does a lot of the bargain hunting:

'He shops for cheap offers…he's good at finding deals, so there's a shop… that's called [name of pound shop] and now they were getting rid of just out of date stock and you could buy 15 things for £1…He'll figure it out… because he's the oldest and he's always seen that it's been like that for us.'

The whole family also goes to Tesco at the end of day; they talk about:

'…picking the right time of day – usually around 9ish – [to find the] reduced items…sausages for 10p and things like that, because we have to, because that's the way that we're going to put food in our cupboards, because of how difficult it is.'

However, the variety and quality of the food can suffer. Cole's mother's menu is restricted to a few dishes such as pasta bake or sausage and mash – '*the two cheapest meals that I always make for the kids*'. She also buys pies and whatever is 'on offer' in the local supermarket. Asked about vegetables, she says: '*I like to do fresh veg and what not. I mean I'm not saying I wouldn't have frozen veg, because it's handy and it's cheap and it's good for making a meal*.' The mother sees herself as a good manager and puts considerable effort into feeding the family: '*We eat healthily and that's not all junk food and what not, so yeah, we do, do all right*.'

Cole's account of his mother's cooking suggests he likes everything she makes and does not consider he is eating other than healthily (Figure 5.6). '*Sometimes we have quick dinners or like pasta bake and that, but sometimes we have long-cooking dinners*.' His favourite meal is pasta bake – '*pasta, bacon and cheese sauce, bacon, because I love bacon, peppers and stuff like that really*' – and he goes on to describe how his mother makes it. His other favourite meal is salad.

However, Cole's mother claims that:

'It does become a bit monotonous sometimes and you do try and think how can we change it a little bit or just think "well you know I'll just have a sandwich".'

They have takeaway pizza once a month which their grandmother pays for when she visits. Cole's mother buys fruit for the children's packed lunches, but it is more scarce outside of term time.

Figure 5.6
Cole's typical school day menu

Breakfast	Cereals, porridge, bran flakes, Weetabix
Lunch	Peanut butter or chocolate spread sandwich, fruit and crisps (packed lunch)
Evening meal	Pasta bake with bacon and peppers, salad including grapes and peanuts
Snacks	Sweets occasionally if has money (rare)

Compromises in food quality

Many families manage to eat enough by compromising the quality of the food they purchase. One of these is Troy (age 12, white British) who lives in the coastal town with his mother and four younger siblings. His mother has never been in paid work and relies on benefits. Both Troy's mother and one of her youngest children have health problems. In the past year, the mother has experienced two long delays in receiving child tax credit following the birth of twins, and she was reassessed for income support. As a result, she has been living on child benefit of around £75 a week. While this is a vital source of income, Troy's mother does not have enough money for food. She has had several food bank parcels, an experience she describes as degrading: '*...you never thought that you'd have to go through something like that, to be able to ask someone else for food for your children.*'

She often borrows money from friends and neighbours whom she repays each week. But then she gets into financial difficulty again, never able to catch up. She has also significant debts to a 'buy now, pay later' home furnishing shop.

Troy's mother prides herself on her cooking ingenuity: '*...when you're on benefits you make a dinner out of nothing.*' She manages to feed her large family by cooking dishes that '*go round for everyone*' – such as stew, sausage casserole or shepherd's pie (Figure 5.7) – and that she expects everyone to eat. However, the meat she uses is of lower nutritional quality – sausage and mince, for example – and meals are 'padded out' with carbohydrates: '*more potatoes, more veg, yeah, rather than the meat*'. She also gets chips from the chip shop. She copes with shortages of food by always having bread in the house: '*then at least they've got toast or a sandwich*'. Fruit, she claims, is not affordable, but she makes sure the children eat vegetables. While she would prefer to buy fresh, '*now I'm having to buy frozen veg just for it to go round*'. On balance, Troy's mother says that, although their diet is not very healthy overall, *'we have good meals'*. In her view, while the quality of food is compromised, no one reports going without enough to eat.

Figure 5.7
Troy's typical school day menu

Breakfast	Troy does not eat breakfast
Lunch	A sandwich (FSM)
Evening meal	Eats anything his mother cooks, including vegetables (does not like); loves pepperoni pizza, nachos, stew, shepherd's pie
Snacks	Toast after dinner, cereal in evening, apple or banana if there are any, crisps

Eating fruit and vegetables

Buying food that is filling rather than nutritious often means cutting back on fresh food, particularly fruit and vegetables. While the UK government recommends eating at least five portions of fruit and vegetables a day, it is known that only a minority of the population achieves this and that purchases of fruit and vegetables in low-income households are much farther from the target than those in households with higher incomes.[7] Analysis of national data from the Health Behaviour in School-aged Children (HBSC) study found that this gradient also holds for 11- to 15-year-old young people in England: 63.6 per cent ate vegetables at least 5–6 times a week in 2014.[8] However, this varied by family affluence status (FAS), a proxy for income, with the proportion at 48.7 per cent for the low FAS group and 64.6 per cent for the medium/high FAS group. As to fruit consumption, the HBSC data found that 45.8 per cent of young people in the low FAS group ate fruit at least 5–6 times a week in 2014 compared to 53.4 per cent for the medium/high FAS group (with an average of 52.9 per cent).

Alongside the interviews in our study, young people were asked to complete the 'eating habits module' from the HBSC as part of a self-completion questionnaire. Just over half of the children who completed the question (26/48) said they ate vegetables at least 5–6 times a week. This is a bit higher than the low FAS group in the national HBSC sample but below the average (63.6 per cent). A much lower proportion of our young people, just over a third of the children who completed the question (17/47), reported eating fruit at least 5–6 times a week – much lower than the average and lower than the low FAS group in the national HBSC sample.

Maddy's grandmother says she tries 'to do one decent meal in the week'. Maddy says her grandmother 'roasts every Sunday'.

Of course, eating 5–6 portions a week is much less than eating the recommended five a day, and is likely to be impacting present and future health.

The children and their parents in our study knew about national dietary recommendations and expressed a desire to buy and consume fruit and vegetables. Indeed, in some families vegetables are routinely eaten as part of a daily soup or stew. However, many find it difficult to purchase as much – particularly fresh – fruit and vegetables as they would like.[9]

Maya (age 15) has learned that blueberries are a so-called 'superfood' and asked her mother to buy them when she was doing exams. However, while Maya knows about health and nutrition, the family budget does not necessarily allow her mother to satisfy her healthy preferences. Her mother manages by buying frozen fruit when she can. Like many, she would prefer to purchase fresh fruit and vegetables but buys frozen as it is non-perishable and, therefore, more economical.

Maddy's grandmother says she tries to cook one 'decent meal' a week but thinks she *'should eat a little more fruit, cos it's quite cheap, fruit'*. However, she notes that this can be a waste of money as it is perishable, *'but when I do fancy one it's sort of like dried out or gone off'*. While she is aware of recommendations for a healthy diet, she buys what she calls 'cheap food' to manage. She thinks that her granddaughter eats a lot of *'junk food'* because *'that's all we can afford'*.

Troy's mother would like her children to eat five a day but says: *'We could eat more salads and more fruit if we could afford it – I can't.'* Ayo's mother, who relies on charity food, mentions a lack of fresh food and the poor quality of the tinned food. She says: *'You know like most of the charities I go, they give us cheap things, you know.'* She has, however, honed her skills to make the most out of what they are given.

Asked about the turkey they were given for Christmas by the charity, Dayo said: 'We had it with cassava flakes.'

Dayo and Ayo live in two damp rooms in a flat shared with two other families. 'In the living room where we sat were two fridges [...] and on top of the little one in the corner was a stack of food, mainly biscuits, all of which she said was from the [charity]. There was a bowl of browning bananas which also came from [charity] because the children like to eat fruit.' (field note)

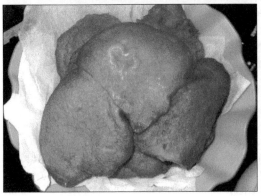

'Akara' (bean cake) made by Dayo and Ayo's mother. Most of the food they receive from the charity is 'English'. She supplements this with items from the local street market that she buys with the little money they have.

Filling food

Alongside the interview, the parents (usually mothers) completed a 'food coping strategies' questionnaire, usually with the researcher or occasionally by themselves. The questionnaire prompted comments about, as well as helping quantify, different ways of managing. Asked whether they buy foods which are 'filling rather than nutritious', of the 43 parents who answered, less than a quarter said they 'never' do, while over a third said they do it 'often' and around the same proportion said they do so 'sometimes'. In their interviews, mothers extrapolated. Dylan's mother says she is more interested in making her children eat what they are given and feel full rather than with nutrition:

> Mother   …I don't really look at [food] groups if you know what I mean. My answer is…if I know that my children are going to eat that, I'll sit and give them the food rather than not, if you know what I mean. So I'd rather do it that way. Yes.
>
> Interviewer   Yeah, yeah.
>
> Mother   And it's about making sure that my children are not going hungry.

Fried plantain that Dylan says may be eaten alone or with 'a bit of stew'.

Parents with low incomes stick to foods that are predictable and acceptable to children; they cannot afford for food to go to waste.[10] Given many children's preferences for less healthy foods and the moral injunction for mothers to feed children well, this can lead to feelings of inadequacy.

Jaivon and Tenisha's mother says: '...some things that I'll eat a lot of and there's some things I won't, and then usually it'll spoil, so I'll get the frozen one instead.'

Shaniya's mother suggests she is highly aware of what constitutes a healthy diet since her son has a bowel disorder. However, her budget does not stretch to achieving this and this causes her to worry: '*I need to be careful of how much starch and carbohydrates I'm putting in my son's body, which doesn't help because this is the food that I'm only able to buy because I can't afford more of the fruits and vegetables that he needs.*' She continues: '*and the thing is [when the budget is tight] I have to cut back on food. I have to cut back on food and just fill my house up with pasta and sauces for pasta bake and I know that if we make two big pasta bakes that will last us two days.*' This has consequences for how she feels about herself as a mother:

> 'And the most things that people are proud of is their cooking or their home you know, and how I see it I'm not proud of either, because I can't cook what I want to cook and cook how I like to cook, because everything's got to be cut down.'

Providing children with adequate food is a central expectation of being a parent. Shaniya's mother eloquently expresses how being unable to give her children the food they need to flourish injures her self-esteem, resulting in a sense of personal shame.[11]

Summary

Around a quarter of the children we interviewed did not have enough to eat; if parents were not sacrificing their own intake to protect their children, the number would have been much greater. In most families, compromises were made in terms of the quality of the food and few were able to buy as much fresh fruit or vegetables as they would like.

For many families, poverty has been directly caused by, or has led to, other challenges such as major life events, lack of social support, illness and disability, including mental health issues. These challenges, plus a very low income, mean that some parents struggle to adequately feed their children. For some families, poverty is a constant feature of their lives and one that they have long become used to. For others, the reasons why they find it so hard to feed themselves lie in the precarity of their lives. Many families have unpredictable incomes, the reasons for which are not accidental but a direct result of welfare, immigration and employment policies.

Feeding the family is an everyday struggle for all the families in the study. Some mothers employ established ways of managing on meagre food budgets. When they have the time, some invest energy and large amounts of their day preparing food from scratch. Others invest time shopping around and buying cheap brands and processed foods: pre-prepared foods are widely available and often cheaper than fresh food, more likely to be filling for, and acceptable to, children, and less likely to go to waste. Nutritionally, frozen and tinned fruits and vegetables may be at least as good as fresh. However, many mothers expressed that they would like to choose a wider variety of fresh fruit especially.

Cooking from scratch can take longer and cost much more because of the need to buy several different ingredients, particularly store cupboard items. Home cooking requires pots, pans, knives, chopping boards etc., which not all low-income families possess, to say nothing of a functioning cooker. Also, many dishes require cooking for an hour or more. Fuel costs can be a problem – reheating cheap ready meals in a microwave is cheaper. Of course, some people cannot cook at all, because of living in hostel accommodation or lacking facilities or because they do not have money to top up their fuel meters. Takeaways and sandwiches act as cheap substitutes.[12]

Shola's mother's pounded yam with spinach. The yam is made from a powder mixed with hot water. The spinach is cooked with meat – drumstick or 'shakki' (tripe). Shola said her mother spent a lot of time preparing food and cooking: 'You'd have to start like the day before and then soak the spinach and make sure it's soft before it goes into the thing...so it's a long process.'

For some families, opportunities for 'shopping around' are constrained by local availability and access including lack of transport, disability, ill health and limited time due to parents' working hours. Other families are reliant on extra-household support from extended family or charities. Most families report being unable to afford as much fresh fruit as they would like. This is noticeably absent from the children's menus and reflected in the much lower than average reported fruit intake of the young people we interviewed. A lack of fruit and vegetables is likely to affect children's current and future health.

Notes

1   R O'Connell and J Brannen, 'Food poverty and the families the state has turned its back on: the case of the UK', in HP Gaisbauer, G Schweiger and C Sedmak (eds), *Absolute Poverty in Europe: interdisciplinary perspectives on a hidden phenomenon*, Policy Press, 2019

2   P Attree, 'Low-income mothers, nutrition and health: a systematic review of qualitative evidence', *Maternal and Child Nutrition*, 1(4), 2005, pp227–40

3   R Lister, *Poverty*, Polity Press, 2004

4   T Ridge, 'The everyday costs of poverty in childhood: a review of qualitative research exploring the lives and experiences of low-income children in the UK', *Children and Society*, 25(1), 2011, pp73–84

5   D McNeish, S Scott, F Sosenko, S Johnsen and G Bramley, *Women and girls facing severe and multiple disadvantage: an interim report*, LankellyChase, 2016

6   See note 4

7   Department for Environment, Food and Rural Affairs, *Food Statistics Pocketbook 2016*, 2017, p48

8   A Simon, C Owen, R O'Connell and F Books, 'Changing trends in young people's food behaviour and wellbeing in England in relation to family affluence between 2005 and 2014', *Journal of Youth Studies,* 21(5), 2018, pp687–700

9   While nutritionally frozen fruit and vegetables are no less healthy than fresh, people see them as less satisfactory. Considerable symbolic importance is attached to 'freshness', even if in practice fruit and vegetables are kept in cold storage for long periods by food wholesalers/retailers.

10 E Dowler and C Calvert, *Nutrition and diet in lone-parent families in London,* Family Policy Studies Centre, 1995

11 R Walker, *The Shame of Poverty*, Oxford University Press, 2014, and see Chapter 5

12 Some food banks regularly now provide parcels which are 'cold'/non-cook food to accommodate.

Six

Children's experiences of school meals

School plays an important part in establishing and maintaining young people's overall diet intake and eating habits, given this is where they spend a large proportion of their lives. But few studies take a holistic view of what young people eat in different settings. This means that linkages between what children eat at home and their access to food at school are ignored.

The chapter examines the part that school meals play in the lives of children in low-income families. It begins by discussing free school meals (FSMs) and goes on to examine the place of school meals in the lives of particular young people. Although the study did not set out to investigate the ways schools organise meals, school policies and practices have emerged as important influences on young people's experiences.

Free school meals

For more than a century, FSMs have been provided to children in the UK 'whose education might otherwise suffer'.[1] Since 2014, English state-funded schools have been required by law to provide FSMs to all Key Stage 1 (reception, year 1 and year 2) children.[2] For older children at state-funded schools, FSM eligibility is linked to the parent (or the young person) being in receipt of certain means-tested benefits.

It has been calculated that around a third of children growing up in poverty do not receive FSMs.[3] The majority are missing out because their parents are working and they, therefore, do not qualify. When the government started rolling out universal credit, all families who moved onto it – working or not – were entitled to free school meals for their children. Had these arrangements continued, nearly all children living in poverty would have been eligible for a FSM. However, the government has now implemented a means test to restrict the numbers of children on universal credit who will be eligible. Analysis by CPAG with the Children's Society suggests several hundred thousand families could be caught by a free school meals 'poverty trap' that penalises them for earning more.[4] However, transitional protections mean that pupils eligible for FSMs on 31 March 2018, and those who become eligible after this date, remain entitled until 31 March 2022, whether or not they or their parents continue to be entitled to a qualifying benefit. Those entitled on 31 March 2022 continue to be entitled until they finish their current stage of education – for example, primary or secondary school.

Some who receive FSMs claim the allowance does not pay for enough food to fill them up and that being on FSMs identifies them as being different. While in Wales and Scotland, legislation requires that children cannot be identified by anyone other than an authorised person 'as a pupil who receives a school lunch free of charge',[5] no such legislation exists in England – although the cashless systems increasingly employed in schools can mean that FSM pupils receive their school meals without the need to identify their FSM status.

School meals policy has seen a series of sharp turns on funding, privatisation and nutritional content and quality.[6] The School Food Standards introduced in England in 2015 endorse a 'whole school approach' to healthy school meals. However, the standards are not mandatory for all schools, implementation is patchy and there is a lack of monitoring. There is known to be a mismatch in some schools between what children are taught about healthy food and the food that is available.

The receipt (or not) of free school meals

This chapter focuses on secondary school children. Except for five who were still at primary school, the children in this study were all at secondary school. The 46 secondary school pupils attended 16 schools: three in the coastal area and 13 in inner London.

Almost all the children lived in households with the lowest incomes. However, reflecting the national picture, FSMs were received by around only half of the families. This was mainly because parents were in paid employment, even though many were in low-paid and/or insecure work. Some were entitled to working tax credit, the tax credit for those in low-paid work, but this is not a qualifying benefit for FSMs. In some cases, the family's immigration status meant they had no recourse to public funds and so no FSM entitlement, since FSMs are paid out of public funds.

In a few families, children did receive FSMs, despite having at least one employed parent, but all were in particular circumstances. In three instances, lunch was provided free by the school (one because the child had a scholarship, and the other two because the school funded lunches for all children through its own budget). In another case, a mother had recently started working but this had not been fully processed and, in another, a mother received a benefit which qualified her children for FSMs, despite her being in paid work.

In the families with no employed parents, most children received FSMs. However, in three families where the parent was not in employment, the children did not get FSMs. In one, the mother had lost her job but was still *'waiting for income support to be sorted'*, and this included waiting for the 'passported' FSM benefit too.[7] In two families, it was because the parents have a 'no recourse to public funds' condition.

While the eligibility for claiming FSMs is set by government, schools' practices – and the experiences of children and families – vary, depending on local circumstances.

Schools' practices

The policies and practices employed by schools influence children's access to, and experiences of, school meals. We learned a lot about school practices from what the children told us, and from interviewing teachers in three schools, as well as the information on school websites. We categorised school meal practices as being either 'inclusive' or 'exclusionary'.

'Inclusive' school meal practices make no differentiation in the lunchtime food available, or the means of serving it, to children from poorer or from better-off families. Indeed, in these schools, food was sometimes an explicit means of including all children into the school community. The children getting FSMs were not publicly identified in any way.

'Exclusionary' school meal practices restrict the food options for children from lower income families, excluding them from adequate meals. Practices, such as being told to 'return food items', identified and demeaned FSM children.

According to our analysis, around two-thirds of the children attended exclusionary schools. Half of these received FSMs and half did not. Less than a third attended inclusive schools. Again, around half of these had FSMs and around half did not.

Free school meals and inclusive school practices

Free school meals are vital to children who are otherwise socially and economically marginalised

Joseph (age 12, West African origin) lives with his mother, a lone parent, in temporary accommodation (a hostel) in the inner London borough. Their income is in the lowest group (see Appendix 1, Table 1.2). The hostel does not allow visitors so our interview, with Joseph and his mother together, took place in a McDonald's. Joseph's mother has lived in the UK for 15 years but has only recently been granted 'discretionary leave to remain' for two and a half years, enabling her to apply for jobseeker's allowance. They currently live on about £130 a week, made up of jobseeker's allowance and child tax credit. For some reason that was unclear, they are not getting child benefit at the moment. Joseph's mother spends £50 a week paying the debts she incurred obtaining her 'papers' (legal status), as well as £70 a month on mobile phones for Joseph and herself. As his mother gets a qualifying benefit (income-based jobseeker's allowance), Joseph receives FSMs. Given there is often a lack of good food at home, this is vital to his wellbeing.

Their food budget is variable but extremely low, usually around £25 a week – just over a third of the Food Budget Standard (see p19). The quantity and quality of food at home is compromised. Joseph's mother cooks mainly West African food, along with some '*British food*' for her son, such as spaghetti bolognese and instant noodles. She cuts up fruit so it goes further and Joseph sometimes takes this to school to eat at breaktime. The mother thinks their diet is reasonably healthy but says that with more money she would buy food that '*would make my boy grow*' and '*something that's good for the brain*', such as a variety of fruit and oily fish, both of which are traditional to her cultural background and practices. When food runs low, they just eat potatoes and bread and butter. Joseph's mother deliberately misses meals, or eats less than she wants, to make sure Joseph has enough to eat, although he, nevertheless, is sometimes hungry too. She has used food banks but is critical of them, saying a lot of the food she was given was at, or past, its expiry date, so she ended up not using it.

Joseph's school is an academy that opened before September 2010 and, therefore, has to comply with the School Food Standards. The school has a 'family service' approach to meals in which no money changes hands and everyone eats the same meal together, including

Figure 6.1
Joseph's typical school day menu

Breakfast	Bread at home, sometimes breakfast at school club
School food	Hot meal (such as chicken curry and rice, macaroni cheese, spaghetti bolognaise) and dessert (such as cheesecake, jelly, fruit, ice cream, cake)
Evening meal	Rice and stew with vegetables, spinach or mincemeat, noodles
Snacks	Occasional packet of biscuits or slice of bread and cup of tea

teachers. Meals cost a set £2 a day. Parents are encouraged to apply for FSMs but there is a recognition that some families are on the threshold of eligibility. We were told that all students eat a meal, regardless of whether their account for meals is in arrears. While the scheme is not economically efficient for the school – it loses money, especially as some students have debts – the school places an emphasis on the importance of lunch and '*make[s] it a priority*'. Since everyone shares the same hot, cooked meal regardless of whether they have paid or are on FSMs, the children are not aware of differences between them.

Joseph eats breakfast every day either at home (his mother skips it) or at the free breakfast club at school: '*if I'm late I don't go, but if I'm early I go*'. At lunchtime, the children are allocated a table of six and each table has a large tray of food, such as chicken curry and rice, macaroni cheese or spaghetti bolognese. Each child has a role in cutting up the food, sharing it out or clearing up afterwards. Dessert is also shared out by the children at the table. At breaktime children are not allowed to bring money or food, except water and fruit, to school. The school provides ingredients for food technology classes and foods made, such as cakes, are shared among the pupils at the end of the day.

Joseph currently has the role of serving lunch and speaks positively about the food at school. Unsurprisingly, given the way in which meals are provided and served, he does not mention feeling stigmatised. '*Everybody gets the same food,*' he says and this is the same for school trips. Joseph feels included and he likes the food.

Given the importance of FSMs, both financially and socially, the school holidays are especially difficult, and Joseph gets hungry and fed up. This was a difficult topic to discuss in front of his mother but, as we know from his questionnaire, Joseph sometimes goes to bed hungry.

Free school meals are important to children of parents in low-paid work

In most families with a parent in paid employment, children did not get FSMs despite being on a low income. However, this was not the case for Kiyana, whose school adopted an inclusive approach to school lunches.

Kiyana (age 12, black British) lives with her mother and younger sister in a local authority flat in the inner London borough. Her mother is employed by the local authority in low-paid care work. She works long hours. Kiyana's father visits daily to care and cook for the children while her mother is at work and he contributes financially by paying child maintenance. Their household income also includes the mother's wages, child benefit and child tax credit. However, they are still in the lowest income group (see Appendix 1, Table 1.2) and there is very little money left after essentials have been paid for. However, Kiyana's mother says she should not complain:

> '...by the time I've got paid and paid out, you know...there's hardly anything left.[...]You know, I could do with some more money, but what can you do, you know. You've got to be thankful you've got a job these days so...'

Comparing their situation favourably to others who are worse off is a way Kiyana's mother makes sense of, and manages, their situation (see Chapter 5).

The family spends around £70 a week on food. This is just under the Food Budget Standard (see p19). Kiyana's mother economises by shopping around and using local 'ethnic' food shops and the street market to buy meat and fish. She says that they are trying to organise a growing scheme on the estate with the help of the tenants' association.

However, she has worried about running out of food in the past and has had to borrow money to pay for food. Their oven has also been broken for the last two weeks but, with no money to spare for emergencies like this, she cannot afford to get it fixed. This means they are currently restricted to the hob and microwave, which limits what they can cook at home. Since the family does not receive a qualifying benefit, Kiyana is not eligible for FSMs.

Kiyana's school's inclusive food policy means no family has to pay for school meals. In recognition that many of its pupils are from employed families on low incomes who are not eligible for FSMs but would benefit from them, the voluntary aided school funds lunches for all pupils from its own budget – mainly by raising income from letting the school buildings when they are not in use. School meals are compulsory on school trips too; packed lunches are provided for everyone by the school:

> '...they have it all in the bags and then they have it on the table, and then you can look in the bags and see which ones you want.'

Kiyana generally likes the food at school and mentions that for people who do not like the hot meals, there are sandwiches, which she has one or two days a week. She does not mention feeling excluded at lunchtimes.

Figure 6.2
Kiyana's typical school day menu

Breakfast	Does not always eat breakfast at home or school, mother encourages hot drink
Food at school	Snack at breaktime, such as muffin and a drink, if she has money Lunch provided for free: hot food such as fish and chips, sandwich two days a week
Evening meal	Meatballs and rice, fish, chicken
Snacks	Biscuits, sometimes chicken and chips if saved money

During the school holidays, when her mother is at work, Kiyana and her friends spend much of their time at the local adventure playground. It is staffed and children can use it for free.[8] They go out to local takeaways and can also make food at the playground's centre, where they sometimes cook in the open air: *'We'll go and get food, like chicken and chips, or like if there was something going outside [...] it would be for cooking.'* Her mother says that the school holidays are hard as the children need feeding as well as money for activities, which *'you know cos obviously it's just extra'*. She says:

> 'I find it...it's a bit more expensive when they're on school holidays cos obviously they're at home all day, so [I need to] have money for that...yeah and the food.'

In working families such as this where there is very little money left over after regular costs have been met, school meals are important for ensuring children eat a proper meal, at least during term time.

Free school meals and exclusionary school practices

Free school meals can be a source of stigma

Murad (age 12, black British) lives with his mother, a lone parent, and sibling in the inner London borough. Murad's mother has not worked for about 12 years as she is disabled, in chronic pain and walks with a stick. They live in a local authority maisonette (previously they lived in temporary accommodation). The household income is made up of employment and support allowance, disability living allowance, child tax credit and child benefit. The family spends about £90 to £100 a week on food – slightly over the Food Budget Standard (see p19), which includes the cost of pre-prepared foods that Murad's mother relies on when she is not up to cooking. Although they have never gone short of food, Murad's mother has sometimes had to cut back on the food budget to meet other expenses. Because his mother receives a qualifying benefit (income-related employment and support allowance), Murad is eligible for FSMs. However, his experience of school meals is not positive.

Because his mother's disabilities restrict what she can do, Murad shares the work at home and is a young carer. In the mornings, he helps his mother make breakfast for his younger sister. He eats cereal if there is time.

Murad is a young carer. He often makes breakfast for his little sister and helps with cooking when his mother isn't up to it. This photograph taken by Murad is of toast with chocolate spread. He says it is 'my sister's toast that I made in the morning'.

The evening meal depends on Murad's mother's health. If she is not feeling well, she uses an ActiFry to prepare chips or chicken or gives the children pasta. Murad's mother says she tries to meet guidelines on fruit and vegetables but struggles due to her health problems: '*I tend to always have fruit in the house. And again veg...most of the time, it is just a packet that you stick in a microwave.'*

Murad sometimes makes dinner when his mother cannot manage it; the night before his interview, he made scrambled eggs on toast for himself and his sister. Another evening he cooked himself a frozen lahmacun (Turkish flatbread).

Murad's frozen Turkish lahmacun, 'it's got minced meat and seasoning and tomato sauce and stuff like that, like a pizza kind of thing.'

The community school Murad attends is subject to the School Food Standards. Its canteen opens at break and lunchtime and has a 'mixed' payment system where prepaid cards are encouraged but cash is accepted. The children have to have a salad either in their sandwich or with their meal, which Murad thinks is *'a good start'* but also *'not very smart, as like children can just leave it'*. He says the FSM allowance is £2.05 but it can only be spent at lunch, not breaktime.

Figure 6.3
Murad's typical school day menu

Breakfast	Cereal or nothing if in a hurry
Food at school	Small baguette or sandwich, biscuits smuggled into school
Evening meal	Chicken, chips, pasta, scrambled eggs
Snacks	Fruit, crackers, crisps, biscuits

Murad is very conscious of the prices – he says they have gone up – and of what is included in the FSM. He says he is forced to 'choose' less substantial items than those available to his peers who pay for their meals. This means he is not only hungry but also stigmatised. Murad explains: '*The bigger sandwiches I can't have, the smaller ones I can.*' Asked whether the sandwiches are labelled, he goes on to say:

> 'The baguettes you can tell in size which one's which. But like the sandwich boxes, the triangle sandwich boxes, one's black and one's brown, and I'm allowed the brown one, not the black one.
>
> 'But thing about the baguettes is that if you're not free school meals then you get to have bigger food...which I don't see why. And also they have cheesecakes, so...but there's like the smaller version and there's the bigger version. And if you're not free school meals you get to have the bigger version, and if you are you have to have the small version.'

Murad understandably thinks this is unfair. He says he occasionally eats at breaktime but only '*when I have money on my account*' which is rare. Like many of the other children who receive FSMs, Murad is given 'top-up' money by his mother so he can buy a snack at breaktime. Murad usually gets £1 a day which he makes go further by purchasing food from local supermarkets and fast food outlets on the way to and from school, saying '*the prices in school are a bit high*' and '*people like to get Oreos and Marylands, cos they're thin packets of cookies, and like they can sneak it in*'. In this way, he and other children economise and circumvent rules about 'healthy' school food.

Although Murad receives FSMs, his mother does not mention the school holidays as increasing food expenditure. Last summer the children went to stay with family in North Africa. To meet the cost of this, she bought fewer treats, like ice cream, and 'traded down' from branded to own-brand foods: '*Maybe as opposed to buying my daughter Petits Filous, I might get her a cheaper yoghurt or something like that.*' More usually, however, she prioritises the food budget and, unlike many other mothers, sees expenses, such as utility bills, as being negotiable with the utility company: '*Luckily obviously, because of my disability as well, I'm a vulnerable so they can't just cut me off and stuff like that. So I know I can work with that a bit, so...*' While Murad's mother's disability means that daily life is often a struggle and brings additional costs, including for pre-prepared foods, to some extent she feels that vulnerability brought on by her disability status accords the family some protection.

No free school meal and inclusive school practices

Compulsory school meals are a strain on a large lone-parent working family

Fahad (age 13, British Asian) lives with his mother and five siblings in the inner London borough. His mother is a lone parent and works 16 hours a week, which means she is able to claim working tax credit in addition to child tax credit, child benefit and housing benefit; she also has her own home-based business selling organic food and beauty products. The family rents a local authority house. Fahad's mother runs a car that she needs to take the younger children to day care and drive to work. Around £150 a week is spent on food to feed a family of seven. This is roughly equivalent to the Food Budget Standard for a large family (see p19). The mother enjoys cooking freshly prepared food but is unable to afford as much fruit and vegetables as she would like and has to cut into the food budget to meet debt repayments and unexpected expenses. Fahad finds the diet at home monotonous, saying it is mostly curry and rice. Taking into account the size of the family, the household is in the lowest income group (see Appendix 1, Table 1.2). However, the children do not qualify for FSMs.

The academy Fahad attends opened before September 2010 and must, therefore, comply with the School Food Standards. The school's food practices are inclusive: as at Joseph's school, school meals are mandatory, there is a 'family-style' service and all children are expected to eat the same meal. But, unlike Kiyana's school, lunches are not funded. Therefore, families who are ineligible for FSMs must pay £2.40 a day per child. While the lack of meal choice makes for an inclusive experience, Fahad's mother says her children do not enjoy the meals and '*they come home most days really hungry*'. This understandably causes frustration and resentment.

The school breakfast club provides free porridge and cereal but, Fahad says, '*stuff like croissants, chocolate buns – those kinds of stuff – costs*'. He says '*breakfast is the most important meal*', but he does not usually wake up in time to eat it at home and rarely has it at school either. He does not usually have the time or money to spend: '*If I'm early to school I will just chill there with my friends. Like, maybe I would get like one of the free stuff, but not really.*' This means he is hungry by lunchtime. However, as he doesn't like the food on offer, he often does not eat then either.

Fahad: 'When I'm bored I tend to eat a lot, and that helps me to like distract myself. If there's fruit then I'll eat it...Fruit and junk, well they both um...they will both go very quick in my family. Cos there's, I think, about nine people in the house – I've lost count.'

Figure 6.4

Fahad's typical school day menu

Breakfast	Does not usually eat; occasionally free item from school breakfast club
Food at school	Eats lunch on Wednesdays and Fridays but not on other days as no choice and does not like meals
Evening meal	Curry and rice
Snacks	Crisps, 'junk food if there is any'

Fahad says there is '*only specific stuff that I like*', for example, chicken and potatoes (Wednesdays) and fish and chips (Fridays). He thinks it would be better if the school worked with the students to design the menus, but is cynical about a recent consultation: '*when I was having school lunches one day, a visitor came in and asked me...he asked me about the food and stuff, and they said how they were going to change it. But everyone knew that he wasn't changing it because he was just a visitor and he never really wrote down anything we said, he just spoke to us about it.*' As a result, Fahad does not expect the meals to improve.

Fahad's mother begrudges having to pay for meals when her son does not eat them and sees them as a pointless expense:

'That's what's killing me as well, because...with the school meals, but I'm arguing the case that my kids don't eat them. They literally sit there at the table and they don't touch their food, so why am I having to pay £12 a week per child for something that goes in the bin? So I'm still arguing that case.'

His mother is in a dispute with the school over dinner money arrears – something that appears to be a growing problem for schools and governing bodies in the UK and which has received media coverage and commentary.[9]

Fahad's mother also finds it expensive to feed the children during the school holidays: '*They want full breakfast, they want full lunch, they want everything.*' She says she has considered getting a lock for the kitchen cupboard to stop the food being eaten too quickly:

> 'Thursday I think I done £140 worth of shopping and by Saturday it was literally half gone. So, I think they're eating out of boredom and just the fact that they're at home and there's food available for them. To a point I really thought I need to get a lock in the kitchen. Once it's done just lock up – you've had your meal. Because they'll just binge eat the whole day.'

Fahad confirms he spends a lot of time eating and that he '*quite frequently*' spends his money on food, especially during the school holidays when he is bored and lonely: '*Cos there's nothing really to do like. When it's on the weekdays you have school to keep you company.*'

For Fahad, then, who lives in an area where he sees few opportunities to get out of the house and socialise, eating is something to 'do', saying '*there's a lot of chicken shops to keep us busy*'. Although he thinks he is overweight and has tried to lose weight, he says it is not easy and that habits are hard to change, especially given there are so many takeaways locally. School food could potentially redress the balance to some extent. However, Fahad's case demonstrates that schools face significant challenges, given many young people's preferences and tastes that are fostered by the fast food industry, and parents' limited resources.

No free school meal and exclusionary school practices

Low-paid parents cannot afford an adequate allowance for a proper meal

Faith (age 15, West African) lives with her father, a widower, and three siblings in the inner London borough. The family migrated to the UK 11 years ago. Like other well-qualified migrants from the Commonwealth educated to degree level, Faith's father is in low-paid employment in an NHS hospital. He works full time. The household income is made up of £1,690 take-home wages plus around £250 a month child benefit for four children. To cope with recent loss of tax credits (following changes made to the income threshold for eligibility introduced in 2016), the father has had to cut back. This includes fewer phone calls to family in Africa and reducing utility bills including, for example, using less gas for cooking. Faith's father has had to borrow money to pay bills and to furnish the flat; the debt repayments are about £300 a month. The family food budget is very low, at around £50 a week for the family of five. This is just over a third of the Food Budget Standard (see p19). The father cooks traditional West African food. He does not eat breakfast so there is more food for the children and takes leftovers to work for lunch. However, because the family does not receive a qualifying benefit, school meals are an additional cost.

Faith's father gives the four children £2 a day for lunch (£10 a week each). Asked whether it would be cheaper for them to have packed lunches, he says: '*I don't have time to be preparing the packed lunch. And you cannot be taking the same kind of packed lunch; I need to be changing…rotating the packed lunch for them.*' School meals are often seen by migrant parents in the study as an important way of acculturating children, exposing them to different types of food than that eaten at home. Given Faith's father works full time and is concerned his children eat a variety of food, school meals are seen as the only option.

Figure 6.5
Faith's typical school day menu

Breakfast	Cereal, toast with butter and jam or sandwich
School food	Hot meal (such as fish and chips and chocolate cake with custard) or snack at break (such as pizza, bacon or sausage roll) plus cold tuna salad
Evening meal	Rice and stew (fish, beef, sometimes chicken), yam, rice, fufu, eba
Snacks	Occasionally a biscuit that the father brings from work or Faith buys from a shop if she saves lunch money

The community school that Faith attends is subject to the School Food Standards. Its canteen sells food and drink at break and lunchtime and has a 'mixed' payment system where prepaid cards are encouraged but cash is accepted. Faith says there is a range of hot and cold food at school at break, including pizza and bacon rolls (£1 per item), and more substantial food at lunchtime that costs around £2. Despite a variety of dishes, she says she doesn't really like the food but '*if I'm hungry, obvi-*

ously I have to eat it'. Faith is highly aware that her circumstances mean she has a lack of choice about what she can buy and eat – especially compared to some of her better-off peers (see Chapter 7).

Faith and her siblings complain that the money their father gives them is not enough. It does not cover food at both lunch and breaktime; at breaktime it is a norm for peers to buy food and when the girls say they feel hungry. As a result, Faith sometimes divides her £2: £1 for break, £1 for lunch. This means she does not eat a proper meal. Like Murad, she says the food at school is expensive compared to the local shops and that the money would go further if she bought food outside school, something she does sometimes. The father lectures his daughters on adapting their expectations to their circumstances; for example, when his youngest complained about the lunch money, he told her: *'You have to adjust. Your sisters who have been in secondary school, the same £10 I'm giving them every week.'* For this reason, he has put a daily 'cap' on the £2. In this way, he says, the family manages. Given the low budget available for food, Faith's father has no option but to keep tight control of his children's spending. While he himself goes without food and Faith feels socially excluded, she does not say that she feels hungry.

During the school holidays, when her father is at work and there is no lunch money, Faith says there is only beans, rice or noodles for lunch. Although this is a time she has worried about having enough food or enough money, this is mainly about not being able to join in with her friends, rather than hunger (see Chapter 7).

Some of Britain's most deprived children are going hungry at school

Emmanuel and Gideon (age 14 and 15, West African origin) have lived in the UK since they were eight and nine years old. They live with their lone mother, who migrated to England 11 years ago, and two younger siblings. Although their mother used to work full time as a cleaner at the local hospital, she is no longer able to work because her 'limited leave to remain' has expired. She is awaiting a decision from the Home Office on her application for 'indefinite leave to remain'. As a result, the family has no recourse to public funds, the mother has lost her right to work and to benefits (including child tax credit and child benefit) and they face eviction. They are at the very bottom of the income distribution and, because they have no recourse to public funds, the children are not entitled to FSMs.

The boys' mother has no food budget currently and was recently referred to a food bank by her GP. She largely depends on a woman she calls 'mother' to help with the younger children and to provide food. While she tries to shop around for bargains, she has no money to spend on transport, and so has to balance travel costs against buying cheaper food further afield. She cooks African dishes and feeds the children with filling foods such as cassava and beans. To prioritise her children's diet, she only eats once a day and does not eat meat. While a varied diet is associated with better health,[10] one of the boys comments on the monotony of the food at home:

> '…keep repeating the same food like over and over and over, just gets boring.
> …We mostly eat rice, that's what we mostly eat.'

The boys' interview begins with them saying they don't eat at school and sometimes not at weekends. One says he has not had fruit for four months; an admission that tells of the extreme hardship experienced by this family.

The boys attend an academy that is subject to the School Food Standards. It operates a cashless payment system and food is available at both lunch and breaktime 'provided the payment card has sufficient money uploaded by a parent' (school website). In two other cases in which families had no recourse to public funds, the schools funded FSMs through their own budgets. However, this required the mothers to reveal their situations which not all parents are, understandably, prepared to do. In this case, the school appears to be unaware of the family's legal status and the mother does not have money to give them. So the boys endure the school day with empty stomachs.

Figure 6.6
Emmanuel and Gideon's typical school day menu

Breakfast	Cereal and milk or rice pudding (sometimes)
School food	Nothing
Evening meal	Rice with stew – tomatoes and sometimes beans
Snacks	More cereal if hungry after school

In the morning before school, the boys say they try to fill up on cornflakes and tinned rice pudding. But hunger affects their performance at school. As one brother notes:

'So I need to have a good breakfast [inaudible] cos sometimes…Monday yeah I was doing an English test and all I could hear was my belly rumbling… it was not enough energy for me to, cos being a test yeah, I was half asleep. Even the tutor came up to me three times saying "Do your test, yeah" and I was so sleepy because…it's difficult and stuff.'

Lack of energy has led to exclusion from class:

'Sometimes you don't have enough energy, you cannot cope in the class-room so you have to like try and rest a bit. You just put your head on the table and you end up falling asleep in the classroom and you get in trouble for it.'

Characteristic of many migrant families, the boys have no lack of aspira-tion; being disciplined for lacking the energy to participate in their educa-tion is especially painful.

The two boys do not eat anything at all at lunchtime. Gideon describes a sense of shame at being forced to watch his friends eating in the canteen:

'It's embarrassing, yeah, you have no money on your card and then you just watch them eat.'

Sometimes he goes to the school library and tries to work instead. Asked if anyone has enquired why he is not having lunch, he says they think he is fasting or doesn't like the school food. When asked about his food pref-erences, he reminisces about the food he used to eat when he was enti-tled to FSMs: '*Sometimes I crave for spaghetti bolognese, pasta and cheese, lasagne.*' Emmanuel describes staying for sports after school despite lacking in energy because of hunger. He told a story about how he suffered a severe pain in his stomach:

'…I can't remember the date but it was like this year, I was so hungry and that, so…all of a sudden yeah it was like…it was like…it was like I got hit on my belly…when I don't eat yeah it comes. Yeah, so I'm scared that it might come back. It was like I got stabbed with a knife and it's still there.'

This highlights not only the physiological sensation of hunger but the psy-chological condition of insecurity that characterises food poverty, not knowing what the future holds or where the next meal is coming from.

In a poignant end to the interview, it became clear that one of the boys planned to spend the voucher we gave them for taking part in the study on buying food for a school camping trip. Every child going on the trip had been asked to bring something to cook: '*I'm going to keep this to buy…like pasta and stuff for my group, because we need to organise what we're going to buy. And sometimes when we talk about how am I going to bring, I say I don't really know how much I'm going to bring. Yeah, so I'm going to save this, then when it comes, yeah, just go and buy pasta, stuff. Hopefully it doesn't expire.*' Precarity and social exclusion defined these children's lives; the devotion of scarce resources towards enabling their participation in this school activity tells of the importance of recognising a standard of living that is more than just survival and reveals some of the hidden costs of the school day.[11]

Summary

Government policies mean that many children whose parents are in low-paid employment and on low incomes are excluded from FSMs. The cost of school meals, therefore, places an additional burden upon scarce household resources.

Children are also excluded because of their parents' immigration status which prevents them from having recourse to public funds. Some schools manage to fund meals for children with no recourse to public funds from their own budgets, but others do not. As a consequence, young people in this group, the most severely deprived children in the country, go hungry at school.

Schools are currently overburdened by the requirements of the National Curriculum, insufficiently resourced and cannot be expected to solve the problems caused by the retrenchment of the welfare state. However, they are well placed to identify which children are in need and their practices can, and do, both reduce and compound social inequalities. Inclusive school meal practices, where they exist, overcome the stigma of publicly identifying children on FSMs. When schools make mealtimes a priority, they can ensure that children are incorporated into the school community through the way they serve food and encourage eating meals together. Such practices mitigate England's national policy whereby children on FSMs are limited to purchasing the food that is affordable from the canteen on the FSM allowance.

In other schools, policies and practices discriminate against children receiving FSMs and publically identify them as 'poor'. Although some children receiving FSMs have positive experiences, others report exclusion, shame and stigma. Many of these children depend on their school lunch for their main meal of the day. Such children, most of whom are growing teenagers, say the allowance of around £2 a day is insufficient to buy enough food to keep up their energy levels. It is also insufficient to cover food at break, a time when they typically feel hungry, especially if they have not eaten breakfast, and when eating appears to be a social norm among young people at school today. Because some children are given money by their parents to buy food at break, this further stigmatises those children who lack money. FSMs are vital for some children in term time. Typically, parents in some low-income families find feeding children in the school holidays hard. Whether or not children have a FSM, holidays are times when demands for food and money for children increase.

Notes

1 L Mason, 'Learning how to eat in public: school dinners', in H Walker (ed), *The Oxford Symposium on Food and Cookery 1991: public eating proceedings*, 1991, p206

2 Section 512ZB Education Act 1996; section 106 Children and Families Act 2014

3 S Royston, L Rodrigues and D Hounsell, *Fair and Square: a policy report on the future of free school meals,* The Children's Society, 2012

4 The Children's Society and Child Poverty Action Group, *The Free School Meals Poverty Trap,* available at www.childrenssociety.org.uk/sites/default/files/fsm-poverty-trap-tcs-cpag-20180312_0.pdf

5 Section 7 Healthy Eating in Schools (Wales) Measure 2009; section 8 Schools (Health Promotion and Nutrition) (Scotland) Act 2007

6 T Lang, D Barling and M Caraher, *Food Policy: integrating health, environment and society*, Oxford University Press, 2009

7 Passported benefits are benefits or schemes which some groups of people are entitled to because of their entitlement to certain other qualifying benefits or tax credits or on the basis of age or circumstances.

8 Most adventure playgrounds in the UK emerged in the 60s, 70s and 80s through grassroots community action in 'desperately deprived areas'. See, for example, T Gill, 'Families need adventure playgrounds, and cities need families', *The Guardian*, 16 May 2011

9 For example, J Monroe, 'What kind of school punishes a hungry child?' *The Guardian*, 2 August 2016

10 E Dowler and C Calvert, *Diets of Lone Parent Families*, Social Policy Research 71, Joseph Rowntree Foundation, January 1995

11 See CPAG Scotland's The Cost of the School Day project at www.cpag.org.uk/cost-school-day and Children North East's Poverty Proofing the School Day project at www.povertyproofing.co.uk.

Seven
Children's social lives

Having friends and socialising with peers is an important part of being a child and teenager. This chapter considers the extent to which young people from the study were able to join in with their peers outside school and the home, when buying snacks and meals from shops and cafés, and whether they could provide hospitality to their friends in terms of offering food or, indeed, accepting such hospitality.

Our interviews revealed a number of constraints on young people's capacity to socialise with their peers and maintain friendships outside school, including and beyond their limited access to money. These include the neighbourhoods they live in, whether there is space to socialise at home, the local food environments and the cost of public transport. For some, being unable to meet up with friends and join in activities resulted in shame and social isolation. Others found ways to socialise despite the constraints.

The local areas: neighbourhoods and transport

Both the inner London and coastal areas had high levels of economic and social deprivation. Associated with this are high levels of crime, which in turn led to a general fear of crime in the communities. Some young people described their local neighbourhoods as threatening places that made them feel unsafe when they were out and about. They said this fear restricted their opportunities for socialising outside their homes.

Shola (age 14, West African, inner London) lives with her mother and younger brother. They share one room of her mother's friend's local authority house, and have occasional use of the kitchen. Because the family has not been granted legal status, despite being in the UK for 11 years, they have no recourse to public funds. They rely on money – about £40 a week – from a church, and a charity for food and clothes. Shola's mother skips meals so there is enough for the children and Shola goes without snacks so that her little brother can have them. Shola does not receive free school meals (FSMs) because of their immigration status. Her mother gives her £10 a week to buy food for school. Shola says she feels very scared of the area, of walking to and from school: '*cos my school's round like the dangerous places. So like there are times when I'm going to school I'm kind of scared about whether what's going to happen when I'm coming back from school*'. This, she says, has affected her friendships:

> 'Like I do have friends, but not tight friends, cos…just cos of the area itself… I'd like to have more friends that I can actually lean on and depend on and tell them things about…but it just happens to be the area, that's why.'

Shola sometimes goes to the food bank with her mother. She says it is 'hectic' and she usually waits in reception.

Most of the food in the cupboards is from charity. Shola's mother says she travels long distances to get food from a charity shop where they also give her £5 for a bus pass. She can use this money to buy other foods that she wants to cook for her children.

Aidan (age 11, white British, inner London) lives in a flat with his mother and brother. Recently, when he was out in a local park, a knife was pulled on him as he was 'rushed' by a crowd of older children. He speaks of his fear of going out and the lack of safe space to play. Troy (age 12, white British, coastal area) is also very negative about the area in which he lives. There had been a stabbing recently: '*[it's] terrible*' and '*anything's better than this place, cos it's just so bad*'. Feeling unsafe in their local environment, as these young people do, profoundly affects how much they – and their parents – want, or are able, to go outside their homes to meet their friends and hang out together.

Nevertheless, some of the young people, particularly in the inner London borough, spoke of the sense of community spirit and cohesion in the neighbourhoods in which they lived. Dayo and Ayo (age 15 and 12, West African) and their mother have lived in London for nearly four years. They live in one room with virtually no income as their mother also has no recourse to public funds. However, they are more positive about the local area; they say that it is an '*accepting area*' and much safer than their environment back in West Africa. Similarly, Jaivon (age 12, black British) who lives in social housing with his mother and three siblings, says that children are 'kind' in the area and that there is a sense of community locally. Kiyana (age 12, black British) also expresses pride in her local area, saying that if you needed help, '*you could ask your neighbours and that's because, like, there it's a really good community and that*'.

The inner London local shopkeeper sometimes lets Fahad pick up food for his mother on credit: 'cos they know us and we come there often, they'll put like a tab for her. And then when she has the opportunity she will pay it.'

Transport

One of the main differences between the two study areas was young people's access to public transport. In the inner London area, as across the whole city, all children and young people in full-time education receive a free bus pass (Zip Oyster card) in addition to being entitled to reduced train and tube fares. Nonetheless, if a pass gets damaged or lost, there is a fee for a replacement, which can be an additional, unexpected expenditure beyond the means of many families on very low incomes. So, for instance, Charlie (age 15, white British) says he is having to spend the little money he has on fares to see a friend because his card snapped, adding that he can't get another one because it costs £10 to replace it. However, in general, having free transport means that children have more freedom to travel than their parents, who are often limited by the cost. Shola's mother, for example, explains that she has to turn down invitations, or rely on the help of friends, as she cannot afford the transport, unlike her daughter:

> '...like one of my friends is doing birthday, so invites me that I should come. I told her I don't have a pass, so she came my house to pick me up. But like my daughter she have free pass, if her friends are doing something she can go. Cos I need to let her free.'

In stark contrast, the children and their families in the coastal area were not subsidised for travel. In this area, young people and their parents complained about the high cost of transport and the lack of child fares on the buses during school hours. As a result, many of these young people were heavily restricted in their social lives. Some described walking long distances to school, or to see friends, and having to set aside money to pay for transport, as Bryony (age 13, white British) explains:

> 'And if my mum don't have the money, I'm going to have to walk to [meet my friends]. And um…it's just a pain to be fair. I mean most of the time we do have money…sometimes actually…but it's just the fact of trying to get places where my friends are. And if they live far away, that's going to take me like an hour to walk there, and then by the time I get there, I'm going to have to spend like half an hour with them and then walk back again.'

Many of the young people in the coastal area had to choose between using their bus money for travel or spending it on going out with friends.

Anna (age 15, East European), lives with her parents and three younger siblings in a privately rented flat. Her mother is currently at home looking after her younger sibling, and her father works 24 hours a week packing food on a zero-hour contract. Because they receive working tax credit, the children do not receive FSMs, and the cost of providing the three school-age children with food for school adds up, at about £10–£12 per child a week.

At the beginning of each school week, Anna's parents give her around £15 to cover the bus to school plus her school lunches. But in fact the bus costs £12.50 a week, so Anna does not have enough for school meals and has to take bread from home. Outside of school, she says her dad sometimes gives her money when he can, to go out with friends to eat, such as to McDonald's, but *'sometimes not, because sometimes we don't have [the money]'*. She manages by setting aside some of her travel and lunch money to enable her to socialise. *'I save my money,'* she says, but she can't always afford to go out with her friends as much as she would like; *'not all the time, not all the time,'* she adds.

Hospitality and reciprocity: eating with friends at each other's homes

Food is fundamental to showing hospitality to guests. Having friends round to play and eat has historically been a norm in the UK, even though current austerity is reducing expectations. While the Poverty and Social Exclusion Survey found (in 2012) that only a small minority of children could not afford to have friends round for tea (8 per cent),[1] this had doubled since 1999, and in the areas we studied we found this to be a more common experience. Less than a fifth of the young people we interviewed report having friends over to eat at their homes and just over a third say they eat at their friends' homes (Table 7.1). Strikingly, of the 20 children who report going to friends' homes to eat sometimes, only half are able to reciprocate.

There were a number of reasons for the restrictions on entertaining friends, such as transport, state of the housing (damp, space), religious and cultural norms, and parental concerns, as well as not having enough money.

Table 7.1
Visiting friends to eat and reciprocating

Eating with friends at each other's home	Number of young people
Visits friends to eat	20
Having friends home to eat	10
Do not eat with friends at own home or friends' homes	21
Total	51

Lack of space at home to invite friends

Some young people had virtually no space at home to welcome others. It was almost impossible for Shola to invite people back to her place, because the family was living in one room, relying on the goodwill of a friend. Similarly, three other young people from the London area were unable to invite friends round to their homes because they were living in hostel accommodation where they were not allowed to have any visitors.

Amara (age 15, North African, inner London) lives with her mother in one large room with a kitchenette and shared bathroom in a very large hostel. They have no income and cannot claim benefits because of their immigration status; they depend on help from friends and the mother doing occasional informal work. The mother explains how living in a hostel was affecting the teenager's friendships and social life:

> 'It's like a prison to my daughter, she's crying all day long, she wants some friends to come over, spend some time with them…but she can't, she can't.'

To give them break from the one room, Amara and her mother regularly take a walk in the local park. Similarly, Joseph (age 12, West African, inner London), who also shares one room with his mother in a hostel, is not allowed visitors other than professionals like social workers. Joseph describes '*window shopping*' every evening in their local area, as an opportunity to get out of their cramped room. Socialising at home for these young people was therefore impossible, and their lives were considerably diminished as a result. It is also clear that these circumstances were not temporary nor a result of policy makers' errors; they are long-standing, and the direct result of policy decisions and practices.

Fahad (age 13, British Asian, inner London) lives with his mother and five siblings. He does not often have friends round because of the lack

Fahad goes to this halal butcher where he gets meat for his mother to save her putting on her religious dress: 'I just quickly jump on my bike, quickly ride there and come back. It saves a lot of time than my mum getting dressed and going out and stuff.'

of space at home. Also, religious restrictions mean that his mother and sisters need to 'cover themselves' if people visit:

> 'Like if my friends are coming over, then it'll probably be a day when like... at least a few people ain't home, because if everyone's home there's like not really any space, like then we're all just cramped up in one room. But usually my friends don't come over, because do you know my mother and sister cover...like then you're not free to the house.'

Cole (age 14, white British, costal area), who lives in a privately rented house with his parents and four siblings, says he cannot invite friends home because of the damp in the house.

The instability of the housing situations in which children live can also inhibit them from inviting their friends home. Connor (age 14, white British) says he cannot have friends round because his mother is still trying to unpack from their last move from one privately rented house to another. As research has noted, repeated moves create anxiety and stress and disrupt children's friendships and sense of security.[2]

Being unable to reciprocate

Amara was was able to visit others but could not reciprocate. She explains how living in a hostel and not having much food mean that she cannot invite people home:

'If I had my own place, my own room, I could say "yeah come over" but my mum [inaudible] I don't have a room, I'm just sharing with my mum. Then we haven't much food so...'

While she goes to other people's homes, she says, '*I just stay with them*'. She can only imagine a time in the future when friends could '*come round and sit with me and actually have fun with me*'.

In another case, Charlie (age 15, white British, inner London) describes sometimes visiting friends' homes where he eats a meal, shares a pizza or tries new food: '*I went to my friend's the other day, had some jerk chicken...his mum cooked it for us...that's the first time I tried jerk chicken...it was nice.*' When asked whether he could ask friends back to his place, Charlie is a bit hesitant in his answer, saying that the food at home was a bit 'basic', perhaps in comparison to what he enjoyed at his friend's home:

Interviewer   What about when people come here, do you feel you can ask people back? And...

Charlie   Yeah, no no, yeah, people have come here, my mum has cooked them food, so it's not that bad. Just like pasta or soup or whatever.

Interviewer   Yeah.

Charlie   Just like basic food. Burgers or whatever.

Inviting friends home did not however always mean asking them to share snacks or meals. Describing a photograph he had taken, Charlie mentions how a friend who came over recently brought his own food with him.

Charlie has pizza from Iceland on a Friday night. 'Friday's when my mum usually gets paid, so there's usually food,' he laughs. His friend came over but he brought his own food (a Chinese takeaway).

In other cases, children whose friends visit say that they do not offer them food as they know their parents cannot afford to feed them. Kiyana (age 12, black British, inner London) says that she does invite friends but they usually leave before it is time to eat. Callum (age 12, white British, coastal area) says that he '*sometimes*' worries about there being enough food when his friends come round; later on in his interview, his mother says that when they eat as a family:

> '…most of your friends stay upstairs though, because they think it's rude to sit around, so I don't have that struggle with him. Cos they've not come down and sat at the table, you think "Oh no!"'

Inviting friends round to her home was often also difficult for Maddy (age 16, white British, inner London). Eating at friends' places can be taken for granted, she thinks, but then she realises how difficult it is for her grandmother to feed everyone:

> 'Like sometimes if my nan hasn't done a recent shop. And if you're at someone's house you don't really take into consideration, you just ask a friend: "Oh, get me this, get me that" and it's like you don't…it's not their fault, you just don't realise what you're doing. And sometimes, it's like, "I don't have the drink or this or that to feed." Like sometimes if there's more than one, "I don't have enough to feed all of you". Or sometimes I tell my nan really late: "Oh can these lot stay tonight?" And I know that's probably really difficult on her, like: "how am I going to feed them?" And if I say "Oh we've already ate" then it's like…it's a relief on her.'

As Ridge has noted, children and young people living in poverty moderate their needs and manage their expectations.[3] Charlie and Callum, for example, appear to accept that they are unable to offer hospitality to their friends, suggesting some of the ways in which the realities of poverty are internalised by young people.

Eating away from home: local food environments, gentrification and eating out

Eating outside the home occasionally is a norm for young people in the UK[4] and a means by which teenagers experience and express increasing autonomy. However, there are tensions between meeting norms for social participation and norms for health, which are heightened where the food environment tends to be unhealthy. Particularly in the inner London borough, a wide variety of foods was available from a diverse array of cafés and restaurants. However, it is also the case that a greater density of less healthy fast food outlets is found in the most deprived neighbourhoods.[5] In any case, the higher cost of more nutritious food generally puts it out of the reach of children and low-income families.

Fast food

Parents in the inner London borough were often critical of the number of fast food outlets and promotion of unhealthy food to young people. Sally's mother mentions children being '*bombarded with adverts*', while Aidan and Sean's mother says the area is saturated with fast food:

> 'This place [food outlets] is all there is. You've got one, two…you've got two pubs, about five takeaways, the Chinese, the chicken shop, Carlo's, Cubana's…The Codfather…and that's just directly there [down the road]. This place is just gross.'

Fahad's mother says fast food ought to be healthier. Faith's father also regards the food available locally as unhealthy and says that his children seem to want to indulge in plenty of fast food.

Fahad says the pictures of curry best capture something about him and his life but so too does what he calls 'English food': 'I would say other food would be English because most of the time…I like English a lot, mostly just the fried stuff from English'… This is a 'lamb doner [burger] with spice inside the seeded bun with some salty chips.'

Jaivon says his mother gives him money to buy 'chicken n chips' and his sister, Tenisha, says her friend sometimes buys them for her on the way home from school. However, their mother says she tries to limit this: 'It's not every day you can eat chicken and chips'.

Kiyana's account confirms the normative place of cheap fast food in the diets of young people in the London borough but notes that this relates to food 'outside' the home. Asked what she would tell teenagers in Portugal or Norway about food and eating in her neighbourhood, she says that *'like most people have takeaways, like most teenagers. Like if they have money and they haven't gone inside like to their house or anything like that.'* Abdul also says that fast food for young people *'depends on your family'* and mentions the role of education. While he also says that lots of young people get chicken and chips after school, he doesn't want to do this because thinks it *'clogs up your arteries...makes your 'blood thicker'*; studying science has made him see it differently. Aidan agrees: *'We have too many chicken and chips shops. We need more healthy shops.'*

 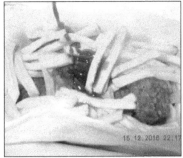

Dayo and Ayo's 'chicken n chips', one with ketchup and mayonnaise and another with BBQ sauce. Asked if it was a special occasion, Ayo says not: 'My mum went out and she just bought it.' Asked if this happened often, Dayo said 'No. It's once in a blue moon.'

Shola, her mother and brother get a box of special fried rice each from a Chinese takeaway around once a month. They eat some and save some. Shola says she prefers takeaway pizza. However, she has pizza at school but not at home: 'Domino's, but we had that once, but it wasn't even with us, it was with the school.' Despite living in an urban area with a large number of cafés and restaurants, Shola has only ever eaten out with the worker from the charity who has taken her for a meal.

Among the young people who have migrated recently to the UK were some from Eastern Europe; some had not yet become used to eating fast food while others were becoming more acculturated. For example, Mariana and Stefan say it is rare for them to have 'chicken n chips'. Roberta reflects that while her friends eat a lot of bad quality food that they buy outside the home, she does not. Anna says her diet has taken a turn for the worse since migrating to UK; she has developed a taste for fast food and eats a lot of it, especially chips. She says that *'in the Czech Republic I'd eat everything, but when I came to England it was difficult, the food and everything, so I stopped eating everything, and now like for five years I eat only chips and the frozen things and that's it.'* Likewise, Piotr says that although he eats well at home he eats too many sweets and sugary drinks *'outside'*.

Gentrification

Both case study areas were experiencing change, albeit at different rates, in their housing stock and local facilities, including shops and eating places, through a process of gentrification. The inner London borough and, more recently, the coastal area were experiencing a growth in expensive cafés and restaurants. This affected the families' access to reasonably priced food shops and, although cheap fast food eating places were still around, the growth in expensive coffee shops and restaurants was, for some, giving them an increased sense of exclusionary displacement.[6]

Charlie (age 15, white British) lives in what is now a more affluent part of the inner London area that has gentrified over the past 20 years or so. He feels restricted by the local food prices and excluded.

Charlie   This high street is really, like, trendy, like. You've got loads of like expensive caffs and stuff. Yeah, it is, yeah…And that's another thing, cos…cos the school's just there on the high street everything's really expensive. So you can't just like go

> with like £2 and buy yourself food. Cos you can't...you can't get like an actual loaf...for £2 around here.

Interviewer   No, you can't. But some of your mates, do they manage to get stuff?

Charlie   They buy, like, paninis and stuff from the cafés for, like, £3, £4...I just don't have that money.

Also in the inner London area, when Amara was asked what she thought about expensive cafés nearby, she explains:

> 'It is harder because I...well, when I go with my friends, for example, Starbucks or Caffè Nero or Costa...you go inside, the coffee's like £5, or... if you take a mocha – £5 – and a cake, it ends up £8. It's not worth it. I mean yeah it might be worth it because the food is nice, but then why would I spend £8 on a coffee and a cake when I could get like proper food?...Like food that can actually last me for a couple of days. There's no point. It affects me, yeah it does...but you can't do nothing.'

Kiyana's mother also says that these places are out of reach:

> 'Um...oh...I suppose it's the budget again, everything's down to money. Some of them are expensive as well, you know, to go and sit in a restaurant and have a meal or something to eat. So...can't really afford it now.'

She suggests that for the same price as a cup of tea and a sandwich in one of these places she could feed the whole family: '*I can buy everything – the tea, the coffee, the milk, the teabags, everything, you know. And the bread and...(laughs) so yeah.*' Jaivon also mentions the cost of one meal being more than it would cost to provide many more meals at home. He does not plan to go to a new café that has opened with £8 salad plates '*cos it's like a lot of money. And then like...and I wouldn't like my mum to spend a lot of money just for like one plate of food for one person*'. Instead, he buys 'penny sweets' from a local shop.

Maddy's grandmother agrees that there are '*too many food shops down there, there's too many*'. However, Maddy has a different perspective. At 16, her tastes have broadened, influenced by her middle class boyfriend. She also suggests generational change:

> 'It's just...it's London, like the whole world revolves around us – it's the language, the diversity, everything, so many opportunities here, I love it.'

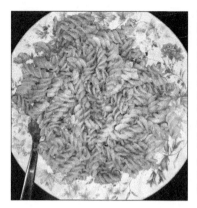

Maddy has been introduced to new foods by her middle class boyfriend. His mother makes her own pesto. 'I didn't actually really know about pesto until my boyfriend's family; they eat pasta a lot and it's an easy dish sort of thing and I quite like it, so I use the basil pesto.' She said: 'Yeah, because I used to eat it there and I told my nan and said buy pesto for me.' For her part, the grandmother said: 'She keeps telling me to get this pasta sauce and tortilla wraps and cheese... Keep going on about it for weeks, drives me mad.'

'A lot of more old people who've lived there don't like it, because you know they've lived there all their life, they don't like the change. But...I don't know, [London borough] has such a bad reputation and it's getting better, so there's nothing wrong with that.'

Phoebe, also 16, is a highly 'reflective' consumer who eats a vegan diet and also likes the diversity and new cafés:

'It's quite mixed. Lots of people like their chicken and chip shops, but they're all...there's always somewhere that has nice food. And like [gentrified local high street market], near to where I live, there's an influx of coffee shops and amazing restaurants and cafés. So, there's no shortage of nicer places to be to eat, so yeah, a wide choice.'

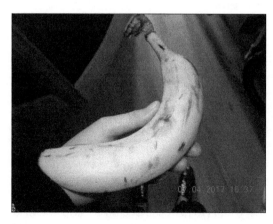

Phoebe says she prefers to buy fair trade bananas. 'Um, I go, actually I go to [cash and carry] market [...] and I get big crates of bananas and they're fair trade. I think it's like £8 for 140.'

Murad, who says some of his friends buy chicken and chips after school, suggests both healthier and unhealthier foods are available:

'I would say that it's well supplied with fruit and veg, and it's also well supplied with sweets and chocolates and unhealthy things. But, all in all, it's pretty balanced.'

Young people had a mix of views, then, about the food available locally and whether they felt included or excluded from the changes that were happening in their neighborhoods as a result of gentrification.

Eating out with friends

Social participation in terms of going out and eating with friends presupposes having the money to spend on food that is eaten out in the street or park, or sitting down in a café or restaurant. We therefore asked the children and young people if they had pocket money or whether they had money to spend on food or leisure activities.

Table 7.2
Money to spend

Type of money to spend	Number of children
Regular pocket money (weekly or monthly)	20
Occasional/irregular pocket money	11
Earns money	2
No money	15
No data	3
Total	51

The national Poverty and Social Exclusion Survey identified regular pocket money as a 'socially perceived necessity' – that is, more than 50 per cent of people surveyed said it was something which everyone should be able to afford and which no one should have to do without.[7] The study found that pocket money was given to around two-thirds (69 per cent) of children. However, just under a fifth (16 per cent) of children nationally were not given pocket money because parents could not afford it. As Table 7.2

shows, around two-fifths of our young people receive regular (either weekly or fortnightly) pocket money from their parent(s), while almost a third do not receive any money at all from their parents or carers (apart from money for school lunches if they do not get FSMs or are given 'top-ups' by parents for extra food or for school travel). So the children in our study are worse off, in terms of having any pocket money to spend, than children nationally. While large numbers of children in the UK are involved in paid work at some time before school leaving age,[8] only two in our study reported earning any money and one of these received earnings from his grandmother for working in her shop.

The young people who receive regular pocket money are given between £5 and £10 a week. A few mention having some money (say, £5) in return for doing chores. Charlie complains that he used to receive pocket money but that it stopped when his mother lost her job. When asked about having some money to go out with his friends, he replies: *'Yeah, I just have to ask and if she has money I'll get like a couple of quid'*; sometimes he says he has to *'keep begging and hopefully money comes'*. As he explains: *'Money is a very important part of life – without money, you can't do a lot of things'*. He says he spends his mostly on *'Food. Food, drink, train travel to go to my friend's house'*. Given the shortage of food at home, it is unsurprising that this is how he spends his money.

A few of the young people say they spend pocket money on buying computer games or going to a skate park or saving towards a larger item. Most, who have money, say – like Charlie – that they spend it on food, whether buying snacks and chips after school or going to places like McDonald's or KFC.

Table 7.3 shows that a third of the young people report eating out with their friends, with a fifth reporting being able to only buy snacks while out with their peers. Just over half the young people were not able to spend money on food with their friends at all.

Table 7.3

Spending money on food to socialise with friends

	Number of children
Eats out with friends (sit down and takeaway, including chicken and chips)	17
Buy snacks only (biscuits, crisps, drink)	10
Do not socialise at all with food	24
Total	51

Amara is one of those who cannot join her friends to eat on the way home from school. Instead, if she has any money, she saves it so that she and her mother can eat food at home. As she explains:

> 'When…well, let's say when she [mother] used to work and give me money I was most of the time there with my friend, but now I just walk home straight away because I can't afford to spend money on…well, let's say food outside. I try to keep and put the money together and just help each other, that's what we do.'

Shola's mother has no recourse to public funds so any money she gives to Shola comes out of the regular donation from a church. She has to use this money to buy lunches as she does not receive FSMs, and the only time Shola can eat out is when she is taken out by a charity worker. '*So I don't feel independent*', she says. Not being able to eat with her friends, rather than with the charity worker, is upsetting:

> Interviewer   Do some of your friends go out and eat and go to cafés and…?
>
> Shola   Yeah that's what…like sometimes that gets me upset – I can't do things like that. Or like I can't do things like that with my friends.

Among the ways in which other young people manage is to juggle their lunch money, but this option is not available to Shola.

Juggling lunch money

As discussed in Chapter 6, some young people are given money by their parents each day for food at school including when the FSM allowance is insufficient. Some of them save this for buying food and socialising outside of school. Kiyana (age 12, black British, inner London), who has FSMs, receives £5 a week from her mother to put on her lunch card for snacks at school but she says that sometimes she saves some of this to spend in shops on her way home from school. Asked how often she goes with friends to get something to eat on her way home, she says it depends on if she has money left: '*I don't do it that much. It's only if I still have money from like when I put money on my lunch cards. If I keep leftover money or if I ask my mum for money so I could use it for any time.*'

Maddy's grandmother gives her £2 each day to top up her FSM allowance. Her grandmother was laid off from her cleaning job and now lives on £130 a week, made up of employment and support allowance, child tax credit and child benefit. She spends about £30 a week on food and skips food once or twice a week when food is running low. Maddy eats with her friends if *'I've got money'* and this depends on whether she has managed to save the money her grandmother gives her each day. She and her friends go to places like McDonald's, Subway and Nando's – *'not fancy restaurants'* she adds. She talks about spending any money she has on food as socialising is important for her, *'so when I go out...I can honestly say that most of my money goes on food'*.

Yet she also talks about the difficulty of spending the little money she has on food when it is, perhaps, meant for other things:

Interviewer How often would you go to those sorts of places [McDonald's etc]?

Maddy See, if I've got money, like I plan to do something and I'll end up spending it on food, and then you realise: 'Oh I should have spent my money on that'. But um...it's usually the weekends when I'm actually going out with friends or...you know, if you're going to someone's house or you go to the shop beforehand and go and get some kebab or something.

Maddy says she makes food and socialising a priority. When asked to summarise her life with regard to food and eating, she emphasises her need to prioritise in this way:

'Um...how would I sum it up? A very social student who...in terms of food, is very free with what she eats. And actually plays a bigger role in her life than she may not notice sometimes. Yeah a lot of my life is spending money, thinking about what I'm going to eat next and prioritising what I'm eating.'

Planning ahead

Some teenagers in the study say that going out with peers means having the money to pay for doing something like going to the cinema as well as buying food when they are out. This causes them difficulties and, in some cases, embarrassment. They are conscious, therefore, that they have to plan ahead, save money from transport or lunch money, or make excuses as to why they cannot join in. Spontaneous socialising is extremely difficult for many. Maddy, for example, was invited to Nando's with some friends on the day of the research interview. She was not able to go because the invitation was at short notice. She explains that, if she had had more notice, she would have saved the £2 a day money she receives from her grandmother:

Interviewer	Like today you said you couldn't go to Nando's because you didn't have the money.
Maddy	No. Uh-uh. But if I planned to save it, I could've.
Interviewer	Could you have done that? Could you have put it aside?
Maddy	Yeah, yeah, usually I just leave it in my pocket and don't spend it. But sometimes if I know I really, really want to save it, I'll put it away. Because if it's in my pocket, I have temptation to spend it.

Making excuses

The stigma and shame experienced by young people and some of the ways they deal with it are discussed in Chapter 8. One strategy was not to disclose to friends and peers the details of their circumstances. Such reluctance to disclose is also evident in the ways that some young people confessed to making excuses for refusing invitations from friends to socialise.

Danisha (age 11, black British, inner London) lives with her mother and helps care for her two siblings, both of whom have disabilities. Her mother has an income of £185 a week, made up of income support, child tax credit, child benefit and disability living allowance. She spends about £35–£40 a week on food and there are constraints on the quantity and quality of the food available. Some of the costs of milk are covered by Healthy Start vouchers. Danisha talks about visiting a cousin's home but does not visit friends. However, she had been invited to a friend's house for a party on two occasions and also to the cinema. On each occasion, she says she 'forgot' to go.

Several young people say they are sometimes invited to occasions which involve both the cinema and eating out and although they may have the money to do one activity, they can't afford both. This means they either have to choose between them and make an excuse, or go to neither. Faith (age 15, West African, inner London) is sometimes invited out with friends.

She usually declines, however:

> 'I'm like I don't really want to come because I have to economise myself… cos you have to go to the cinema and go to buffet, so have to pay for both. And I'm like I can't pay for both, I don't really have enough money for myself to pay for both.'

Like many of the other young people we spoke to, Faith wants to keep this to herself: '*I don't want to show them that, no, I don't have enough money. I say to them "no, I don't really want to come".*' When asked why she says this, she replies:

> 'Because I don't want them to see me as this person that is poor. And I say like I'm not poor, just like…for this time I don't have money to go out.'

As we discuss in Chapter 8, children often conceal their poverty from others.

Sharing and reciprocity

While the children in the study are limited in the money they have to spend on snacks and food outside school, young people engage in a culture of reciprocity and sharing, albeit within limitations. Bryony (age 13, white British, coastal area) says her friends sometimes, but not always, share some food with her:

> 'Well if my friends…sometimes they'll have money and sometimes they'll get me chips or they'll just get me something, which is all right cos they're nice friends and stuff. But sometimes they can't because it's like their money.'

Charlie regularly goes to the local skate park with his friends. He cannot usually eat with them because he lacks the money. On the day of the interview, he was just about to go out. The interviewer asked whether he would buy any food when he was out. He says only if his friends buy him something:

Interviewer	…will you be able to get anything now?
Charlie	No, unless my friends buy me something, no.
Interviewer	Do they do that sometimes?
Charlie	Yeah, sometimes yeah, they buy me…yeah they do.

His friends buy him food like chicken and chips, or a snack, such as crisps or a drink. However, their generosity has limits: *'[they buy things] but not all the time, they don't just like blow out all their money…they ask, "do I like want anything?" or I ask them and "I'll pay you back".'* When asked if he is able to pay them back, he says, *'yeah, eventually, yeah'*. His friends, who tend to be older and earn some money, appear to show understanding of his predicament: *'they know, they're like…they just tell me pay it back when you can…cos they know that I don't have a lot of money so…'*.

Jordan (age 15, white British, coastal area) lives with his mother and older brother in a small privately rented flat. His mother is currently living on about £100 a week from jobseeker's allowance and child benefit. Due to an ongoing dispute, her tax credits have recently been stopped. She spends £30–£40 a week on food. In order to feed herself and her two sons, she regularly relies on a food bank and food from friends and neighbours, who she does small errands for in return.

Unlike some of the children living in more mixed neighborhoods, Jordan says that none of his friends go into shops on the way back from school as none of them have any money. If a friend asks him to go out, he usually can say 'yes' but then adds that he cannot *'really ask'* his mother for money. When he goes out, his friends *'will usually just buy us something and like I'll give them back a bit of money next time I see them'*. He also talks about pooling money to share food with friends in McDonald's: *'When we've all had a couple of quid on us and we've all chipped in together to get something from McDonald's or something to share, like a burger each or something and we've all chipped in.'* That they are all 'in the same boat' seems to make this easier.

Maddy also talks about friends sharing and helping each other out but, like Jordan, she stresses that this is with people who she knows are also struggling with money:

> 'So when I'm with them friends [ie, ones with little money] we help each other out – if she doesn't have any money on her I'll buy her a drink or whatever. Like it's just like little things that you do for each other.'

This sharing and reciprocity with people who also have little money is also important to Maddy:

> 'It's nice because you don't feel uncomfortable and you don't feel like you're going to be judged or anything like that. I know if I don't have any money on me, and my friends did, it'd be like: "I can't have the money, I don't have it, I'm broke"…it'd be like: "it's fine, just let me get it for you." You don't even…

it's got to the point where…you don't ask for that person to pay you back because you know when I've got the money and she hasn't, I'll do it for her. So, whereas when you've got someone with loads of money, it's like: "I'll pay you back. I'll pay you back". So it's quite difficult sometimes.'

While reciprocity provides Maddy with a sense of mutual understanding and solidarity with her peers, it is clear that it entails some delicate negotiations.

Feeling different and left out

In other cases and at other times, however, young people were excluded from the social lives of their peers. This had consequences for sustaining friendships as well as how they felt about themselves. Some admit in the interviews that they feel different from their friends and 'left out' when they cannot take part. Maddy compares herself with other young people, her peers and friends, who have what she calls 'allowances'. In contrast, *'my set money is my school money'*; this is the money her grandmother gives her ostensibly for money for food while at school. *'Generally people always have more money than me'*, she adds. Similarly, Charlie says many of his friends at school have more money than him: *'I'm not saying they're like rich, but they're…both their parents have jobs and stuff.'* Faith compares the money she has with that of her friends at school: *'They don't have a limit. Their parents give them the amount of money they wish to get, so it's different from me.'*

Bryony is also acutely aware of the differences between her access to money and that of some of her friends. She says that one her friends is given £10 a day for lunch that he spends on the way to school on *'crisps and drinks and whatever he wants'*. She herself is sometimes given a pound by her mother to buy a drink or a *'flapjack or something'*. She sometimes meets her friends at places like McDonald's but she rarely has the money to buy her own food; she says her mother gives her money *'whenever she can'*. She confesses that *'sometimes it's hard'* not having the money to join in with her friends and she goes on to suggest, without quite saying, that she feels left out:

'It's…I don't know really, to be fair it's…don't know…I mean it's like they get all that and I have to be, like, there while they eat all their food or they get what they want. And…I don't know…'

As we discuss in Chapter 8, the difficulty with which some young people were able to articulate their feelings reveals something about the sensitivity of the topic of social exclusion as well as the lack of available discourse to describe their experiences.[9]

Emmanuel and Gideon (age 14 and 15, West African, inner London) are in a family with no recourse to public funds and, therefore, no FSM entitlement (see Chapter 6). Consequently, both boys experienced hunger, especially at school. Socially, they describe feeling left out. Sometimes their friends buy chicken and chips after school but when asked if their friends share what they buy, one brother says, '*it's only if they want to give you like a bit, cos it's theirs, only a little bit*'. Asked how this makes them feel, shame and exclusion are clear:

Interviewer	And do you feel awkward cos you can't buy them something back?
Emmanuel	Uhuh.
Gideon	Feels like I'm left out of the fun that happens and stuff. Like it just makes me feel empty.
Emmanuel	It makes me feel, like, what have I done? Like, what have I done?

Shola (age 14, West African, inner London) says she is aware of some young people coming from affluent homes and frequenting expensive restaurants. She says this makes her feel 'different': '*I do have quite a few friends like that. They'll tell me about it and I'd feel left out a bit. So I just like nod and smile, probably walk away or something…it makes me feel different.*'

She also says that a friend '*makes up stories*' to tell other people at school about places they have been to, to keep up the appearance of participating, although Shola knows these stories are not true:

'Like most of them hide it, so…they might fake a story about them going out or something. I have a friend that does that…they might fake a story about them going out. And people believe it cos obviously they don't know it. So… it's like you wouldn't really suspect who's like you and who's not. Cos people are just trying to fit in and not get picked on for the way they live or the way their lifestyle is.'

Shola summed up many of young people's experiences of social participation in their local areas and in relation to food and eating and points to the need to learn quickly to manage money and 'to take care of yourself' fast:

'It's just hard, at some point it's hard. But then like after a while you know it's going to get easier. So…like if you pay attention and stuff it gets easier. But you've just got to learn to be careful. It's like you've got to grow up a bit too fast…so you've got to learn to take care of yourself, learn where to go, where not to go, learn how to manage money and where to buy food and stuff like that. And to learn to keep yourself to yourself.'

According to Shola, learning not to reveal too much about your situation to others is part of growing up in a family without enough money.

Summary

This chapter paints a stark picture of exclusion from consumerised child-hoods[10] and how children, particularly in low-income families, look to consumer culture to establish a sense of belonging[11] as they move into their teenage years. It shows how the neighbourhoods in which they live, and the food outlets they can afford to frequent, shape young people's consumption patterns. Fast food is cheap and popular, but ongoing gentrification means that, although more varied and more nutritious food is now available where some young people live, its cost and the types of establishment largely puts it out of their reach.

Offering hospitality to peers at home and buying food to eat outside home are significant ways in which young people learn to make sense of their place in the world and learn how to build relationships. Being short of money means that, for many young people from low-income families, their social lives are limited and lacking in spontaneity. In order to take part in social activities with their friends, they have to be constantly thinking ahead and setting aside money which was meant for transport and their school lunches so they have the means to meet their friends outside school. They not only have to learn to manage the limited money available to them but also to manage what others know about their situations.

Critically, being unable to be part of a group of friends who socialise around food makes young people feel left out and different. They often feel they cannot tell their friends why they cannot meet up or join in, because they are too ashamed, or do not want to embarrass their parents. Some are able to share food bought outside the home with their friends. Often the act of sharing food or money appears to be offered by peers without a need to discuss or even feel the pressure of reciprocity. However, the sharing of food is restricted and young people feel uncomfortable about what they consider to be taking advantage, especially if they think that reciprocating at a future date will prove difficult.[12]

Notes

1   S Lansley and J Mack, *Breadline Britain: the rise of mass poverty,* Oneworld Publications, 2015, p45

2   S Nettleton, 'Losing a home through mortgage repossession: the views of children', *Children and Society*, 15(2), 2001, pp82-94; T Ridge, 'The everyday costs of poverty in childhood: a review of qualitative research exploring the lives and experiences of low income children in the UK', *Children and Society*, 25(1), 2011, pp73–84

3   T Ridge, 'The everyday costs of poverty in childhood: a review of qualitative research exploring the lives and experiences of low income children in the UK', *Children and Society*, 25(1), 2011, pp73–84

4   L Hamilton, *Young People's Food and Eating Practices: a comparison of higher and lower income households in a London Borough,* PhD Thesis, University College London, forthcoming

5   P Greenfield, 'Poorer areas of England have more fast-food shops, figures show', *The Guardian*, 29 June 2018

6   R Atkinson, 'Losing one's place: narratives of neighbourhood change, market injustice and symbolic displacement', *Housing, Theory and Society*, 32(4), 2015, pp373–438

7   G Main and J Bradshaw, *Child Poverty and Social Exclusion: final report of 2012 PSE study,* Poverty and Social Exclusion in the UK, 2014

8   P Mizen, A Bolton and C Pole, 'School age workers: the paid employment of children in Britain', *Work, Employment and Society*, 13(3), 1999, pp423–38

9   E Ardener,'The problem revisited', in S Ardener (ed), *Perceiving Women*, Dent, 1975, pp19–27; M DeVault, 'Talking and listening from women's standpoint: feminist strategies for interviewing and analysis', *Social Problems*, 37(1), 1990, pp96–116

10 T Ridge, *Childhood Poverty and Social Exclusion: from a child's perspective,* Policy Press, 2002

11 AJ Pugh, *Longing and Belonging: parents, children, and consumer culture,* University of California Press, 2009

12 See also A Knight, R O'Connell and J Brannen, 'Eating with friends, family or not at all: young people's experiences of food poverty in the UK', in W Wills and R O'Connell (eds), *Children and Society*, Special issue: 'Children's and young people's food practices in contexts of poverty and inequality', 32(3), 2018, pp244–54

Eight

What children say about poverty

This chapter is about children's experiences of poverty and who they hold accountable for making sure they can eat properly. First, we focus on how children and young people feel about and manage the experience of poverty and low income and being seen to be 'poor', including not having enough money for adequate food. Second, we present their responses to the question of who should be responsible for ensuring that children have enough good food to eat.

To gauge how young people felt about poverty and food poverty, we asked children a variety of questions towards the end of the interviews, and, when appropriate, we asked them whether they thought money was ever a worry for their parents; whether they ever worried about money or about their parents; whether they talked to others about any worries they had and, if not, why not. We were very careful in our questioning because we know that owning up to poverty is a potentially shaming experience. It is possible that, because of the potential embarrassment, young people under-reported negative feelings.[1] In addition, there are methodological issues concerning power inequalities about asking young people direct questions that can put them 'on the spot', especially when they, as minors, are confronted by adult researchers who do not apparently share young people's disadvantages. Nevertheless, young people often did share their views, and we discuss them here under different headings that reflect our interpretations of what they said.

Experiencing food poverty

Practices of concealment

As we discussed in Chapter 5, children in around a quarter of the families in the study admit to going to school or to bed feeling hungry because there is not enough food at home – always, often or sometimes. Mothers (and, where present, fathers) were quick to assert in their interviews that they go to great lengths to protect their children from the effects of their circumstances by going without food themselves so that children may have more. They also often say they hide the difficulties they have in providing enough food for the family.

Addo (age 12, West African parentage, inner London) lives with his parents and two siblings. He worries that his parents will run out of money and food but suggests that he is protected from knowing the details saying, *'they don't talk to me about it'*. However, from his mother we learn that the family has been through very hard times. His mother was only given leave to remain in Britain five years ago, until which point the family was largely reliant on food parcels from the Red Cross. Addo's mother now takes a positive view of their improved financial situation, especially since her husband is now working: *'It was really...it was so bad, but you have to be positive and look at the positive side, even when things are not the way how they are supposed to be, yeah.'*

Just as Addo's mother conceals hardship from her children, several children also withhold information from others outside the home about the difficulties their families are going through. In Addo's case, he is still quite young but has some awareness of how difficult things are for his parents. Although Addo understands his mother's protective approach, he does not talk to his friends about the family situation. Addo worries about his parents and money but does not talk to them about it. Nor does he feel able to talk to anyone else. As Goffman suggests, by 'avoiding overtures of intimacy the individual can avoid the consequent obligation to divulge information'.[2]

Rejecting the poverty label

Some children make it clear in their interviews that they do not consider their families to be poor or suffering from 'food poverty', even though it is evident from their mothers' accounts that the families have major constraints on their budgets. An example is Bertie (age 11, white British, inner London) who lives with his mother on a council estate. His mother is a carer for members of her family and has always been reliant on benefits for her income. Bertie rejects the idea that there is any shortage of food at home, which is confirmed by his mother's account. Bertie boasts: *'I'm never poor, we eat pie and mash, fish and chips is our thing.'* He also rejects the suggestion that some local people are short of food. Indeed, Bertie is rather unsympathetic to people who are poor and considers that they are pretending not to have any money.

Jordan (age 15, white British, coastal area) lives with his mother and one sibling in a one bedroom flat. They also rely on benefits for income. Jordan expresses ambivalence about being seen as 'poor'. He says that his friends are no different from him: no young people he knows have money to spend on food when they are out and about. He is also keen to dissociate himself and his friends from being seen to be 'really poor':

> 'Like, they may not be, like, poor poor, but they are struggling with the hard times.'

Later he admits that he and his family are 'poor' – '*to some extent, yeah*' – but again tries to distance himself from being what he calls 'poor poor'.

> 'Because we're not poor poor, but we're not like totally like licked with money either, like we are still struggling along like the rest of them, like everyone else.'

This positioning reflects Jordan's negative view of the state of Britain at the time. The interview took place shortly after the British electorate voted to leave the European Union in an area of the country where support for UKIP[3] and for leaving Europe was very high.

Jordan	This country needs to buck its ideas up or it's going to be gone…first we need to stop relying on our parliament so much as well. They can't, they won't always be here to fix everything, so…
Interviewer	Mm, who else could fix things do you think?
Jordan	I don't know, but it's definitely not who's in charge now.

Being positive

Another related strategy for resisting the label of being 'poor' is to be positive about one's own situation and to see others as worse off. Fabien (age 14, West African parentage, inner London) lives with his mother and two siblings. His mother lost her job because of an accident at work. Although his mother is struggling, and has recently used a food bank, Fabien says he has not heard of food banks, perhaps indicating that his mother shields her children from the knowledge that she has used one. However, Fabien admits to going to bed hungry 'sometimes' and also mentions times when there is little food. Yet he regards his family as better off than some 'other people' who are poor:

> 'I would say it's all right, but you have a hard time sometimes. But, yeah, it's not that bad compared to some other people's lives, homeless people and stuff…kind of like where the fridge is empty, there's nothing to eat, and mum has to go and borrow money so that we could eat.'

Fabien plays down the number of times there is not enough to eat at home and maintains an optimistic attitude: *'When there was no food in the cupboards whatsoever to have anything and you just have to hope like mum said.'*

When the young people were asked whether they worried about having enough to eat, a few admitted to having concerns, but they were generally positive about dealing with the issue. Kiyana (age 12, black British, inner London) lives with her mother and sibling. Her mother works full time. When asked if she worries about money, or worries that her mum does, Kiyana says she does not worry. She seemed to be accepting and understanding of the financial constraints on the family. For instance, she says that if she asks her mother for money and is told there isn't any: *'Well I don't know how to explain it…cos like I'll ask her, if she says I don't have any money, I'll just say, "Okay then" or something like that.'* Furthermore, she dismisses the lack of variety of food at home as being a problem, rationalising that it is just that there is nothing she likes: *'like if the things that I like is not here and I feel a bit hungry, and then like…and then if there's nothing then I will just leave it and then I'll just wait.'*

Phoebe (age 16, white British, inner London) lives with her parents and two siblings. This middle class family is currently on a low income because the father's job was made redundant two years ago. The mother works part-time for a charity. Their circumstances illustrate that poverty is not a permanent state and that a single event can propel a family into poverty.[4] The family also demonstrates how the incomes of middle class families can be constrained as well as families living on long-term social security or without recourse to public funds. While Phoebe's family has some assets (they have income from a rented property which covers the mortgage on their home), their income is currently greatly diminished. Unlike many of the young people, she expresses confidence in the family's future believing that her father will get a job soon:

> 'Yeah. I think it definitely is because my dad hasn't had a job for a couple of years now, so that's quite tricky. We have a rental property, so that's really

Phoebe's pasta with spinach: 'This is one of the sachets of pasta that we get from Tesco, that we recently discovered and they're only 20p [...] They are so, so good and they don't have any kind of scary ingredients or nasty ingredients, which is amazing'. The spinach is cooked with garlic and lemon.

good. But I think it's definitely a concern of my parents; it's also a concern of mine, but I think we'll be fine. We're not at a point where "Right, we're not going to be able to get food this week", we're just "Okay, we're not going to be able to do this activity this week" – which I don't have a problem with. I mean it would be nicer to have a bit more cushion so to speak, but yeah, I mean there's nothing you can do about it really...yeah, I think it'll be fine.'

Phoebe empathises with the pressures that low income places on her mother's ability to feed them all: *'I think my mum does definitely [worry about money]...I think she's got a lot more pressure on her now. She's only working [at the charity], and it's not a lot for five of us who inhale food. [laughs] So I'm sure that's difficult.'*

Being proactive

Some children are proactive in combating the food poverty of their families. For example, Fabien admits to some concern about the family not having enough to eat and says he tries to 'save food': *'Yeah, sometimes. Like when I can see that like the fridge is getting empty and I know mum doesn't have money. Like, I try to save food.'* Abdul (age 14, British Asian, inner London) lives with his mother and two siblings. Abdul admits he sometimes worries about the family not having enough money for food but talks about looking *'for food in different shops to compare prices'*. The large family buys in bulk and goes shopping together, typically picking and choosing different items in different supermarkets on the basis of cost.

Normalising hunger

Another way of managing is to normalise hunger – that is, to understand it as part of everyday living and experience. Jimi (age 14, West African, inner London) says he sometimes worries about money, but asserts he is happy with the amount of food he receives at home. On the other hand, elsewhere in the interview he says he occasionally goes to bed feeling hungry. However, he attributes hunger to his recent growth spurt rather than to low income:

> 'I think I just started growing like. I used to be extremely short, but now I'm just averagely short now. When I started to grow I think my belly started to grow as well. And so like eating, so, when I used to have just two slices of toast in the morning, but now that I'm growing up I have to have three slices of toast or else I wouldn't be full. And I would be extremely hungry, tired, and I wouldn't be able to do what I normally do.'

The idea that children and young people, especially boys, are 'always hungry' was fairly common in the interviews with mothers. It is, in one sense, normative, that is 'what people say'. But it also reflects the reality that static or reduced incomes cannot keep up with the growing needs of growing children. As the mother of Fahad (age 13, five siblings), said:

> '…as they're getting older your money's the same, but the kids' needs get… you know I can't feed my kids a few pieces of chicken like I would then when they're all young – I have to make sure the pot's full. You know their needs have got more as they've grown…they're big men now, my boys are like 6ft, 6ft 2, their diets are, you know…but the money's just stayed the same.'

Children develop larger appetites and eat more as they get older.[5] If parents lack the money to afford higher food bills, it is likely that they will not have enough to satisfy their growing needs and will be hungry.

Feeling looked down upon

A few children speak at length about the shame of poverty. In this next example, the young person internalises the shame of poverty as well as describing how other children shame her. Maddy (age 16, white British, inner London) lives with her grandmother who has brought her up. Her grandmother lost her job as a part-time cleaner and is reliant on child tax

'This is a pizza I had at my friend's house...I think it's from Iceland, because I think they recently started selling Dr. Oetker [branded] pizzas.'

credit, child benefit and disability benefits. Maddy worries about lack of money. She also explains how some of her friends refuse to eat certain foods when they visit her because they are 'value' foods (that is, low-cost supermarket own brand) or purchased from Iceland. Maddy finds such situations 'embarrassing' and 'awkward'. She is very brand conscious and careful to add that her grandmother buys a mix of branded and unbranded items:

> 'It's more of you feel embarrassed that you don't have what they're asking for, and then it's kind of like...I don't know, maybe noticing like branded things, if you buy branded or not...when people pick up on that...like my nan does buy branded things, but randomly out of the blue she'll buy something...maybe if she did a shop and she didn't have that much money on her at that time, she'll buy something that's not branded. So, we have a mixture of both; we don't just buy everything that's cheap or...but sometimes if you saw Tesco Value up there, people think "Oh..." and it can be quite awkward sometimes.'

As Allison Pugh suggests, consumption is part of an 'economy of dignity' in which access to consumer culture is a key means of establishing status and acceptance for young people.[6] It also acts as a demonstration that they are sufficiently cared for by their parents.[7] In general, Maddy tends to distance herself from others: she says she does not talk to other people about her life, especially her more affluent friends. Since she lives with her grandmother she particularly avoids talking about her mother to other young people and, if they ask about her, changes the subject.

Being unable to afford the fashionable brands of consumer products is a significant issue for young people when they are at school, as Faith, age 15, explains. Faith lives with her three siblings and her widowed father who is in a low-paid public sector job.

> 'In school it is [a problem]. If you don't have enough money…like if you come to school and you don't have the latest shoes you'd be told like…you'd be like said that "Look at your shoes, look at what you're wearing" or what you're doing this…like you'd be bullied for everything you have.'

Faith goes on to explain that she has learned to speak up for herself at school to deal with teasing and bullying about her clothes:

> 'But like it started to stop when I found the zeal inside of me to say…if I don't speak up then they will continue to do that, if I do speak up they will stop doing that…which now I'm finding the courage and confidence in me to be able to do that – which is stopping them from doing it little by little.'

Faith compares herself negatively with her friends who have more money: *'The friends that I have now, they kind of have like everything they have – they have cousins who gives them money, their dad gives them money, their mum gives them money…their aunties give them money, so…'* In the inner London context in which schools were mixed in terms of social class, this difference was acutely felt by those who lacked money.[8] Being brought up in poverty in a very unequal country like Britain contributes to children's painful experiences.[9]

This next example is of a young person whose family has no choice but to seek help from charity, in particular food banks. Amara (age 15, inner London) lives with her mother in a hostel. They have no income because of their immigration status. She suggests that being dependent on charity means having to be grateful and points to the loss of dignity and human rights in having to depend on such provision. Discussing the food bank that she and her mother visit, Amara says:

'...when I'm hungry I can eat [inaudible] I don't care if it's three months' old [inaudible]. When I'm hungry, I'm hungry and I'm not in a position...I mean I can't complain at the moment, I just can't complain. I'm not in a position to do that.'

Amara is aware of social inequalities as well as the sense of indebtedness that charity places on its recipients:

'We're all human beings and we all should be the same but...I'm not saying it's discrimination...some people kind of get to get everything in life, but we have to cope with what we have, and you can't complain. Because if you complain about it [inaudible] when you really are in need.'

A couple of children refer to the way people living in poverty are negatively portrayed in the mass media, for example, in TV programmes such as 'Benefits Street'. Maddy commented: *'People look down on people like that [being on benefits] all the time and some people genuinely can't help it.'* To counter this, she compares the UK positively with the USA, pleased that Britain has benefits and a healthcare system: *'I like that we have help, I like that we have benefit.'* But she is unhappy about the way people on benefits are treated by the media: *'it's bad, it's not fair'.* Her evaluation reveals a sense of injustice that is also reflected in children's accounts of who is to blame.

Attributions for food poverty

Towards the end of the interview we asked young people: 'Who do you think is responsible for making sure children and young people have access to enough good food?' Given the abstract nature of the question, prompts were sometimes supplied, for example, concerning family, government, charities. In these cases, the prompts may have influenced children's responses. Both interviewer and interviewee tended to move between posing or answering the question normatively (as in whose responsibility it should be) and framing it in terms of practice (whose responsibility it is). A few young people found the question difficult to answer and, in some interviews, the question was not asked. In other cases, children mentioned during the course of the interview who they saw as responsible for ensuring they had enough to eat, or who they blamed for the situation in which not everyone was able to eat well.

Children had a range of views. The three main themes of their responses were 'families' (in concert with other agencies), 'government' and 'social inequality'. In addition, several young people mentioned the role of schools and a couple blamed food manufacturers, and cheap food outlets in particular, for making unhealthy food so readily available. Three children mentioned God. Omar (age 15, West African origin, coastal area) says: *'Because we leave everything to Him, He might help you get food.'* Asked if he ever worries about money, Jimi (age 14, West African origin, inner London) says:

> 'It's something that I try not to think about too much, and I believe that…I believe in God that He will always provide, and I guess that's what my mum's been telling me as well, that God will always provide for us. That's what I try to believe in, and so far nothing [bad] has happened, so I choose to believe in God because of that.'

However, about a quarter saw providing enough good food for children as the responsibility of parents, while about a quarter held the government accountable. Most children employed a language of moral responsibility, especially those who blamed the government for not providing families with enough money to eat properly.

Families working in concert with other agencies

About a quarter of the young people say parents should be responsible for ensuring their children have enough to eat. However, they do not blame them when this proves difficult. They simply consider it a given that parents are the main persons charged with this responsibility. In times of hardship, however, young people expect the government to take responsibility and they also note that schools have a role to play.

At the time of the interview, Dayo and Ayo's family (age 15 and 12, West African, two parents, inner London) was facing destitution because of their lack of legal status. The two boys often lacked sufficient food. They take the argument about government responsibility to its logical conclusions:

> Dayo   Family is the power of love and family is the power of team. And, secondly, the government is – I said the government because government is the one that takes care of like the hospitals and the charities and, well, not really charity, but would

control, yeah. So, I think the government should be probably monitoring what is going on.

Ayo I think the parents because of what he said, and government because if a child dies the government is always serious about it. So, [even] if the child doesn't die they should still be serious about the child anyway.

Attributing responsibility to those in power does not mean that children were dismissive of people (adults) taking responsibility. On the contrary, several children talk at some length about the importance of morality – of people 'doing the right thing' and not spending on 'what you don't really need'. Asked whose responsibility it is to ensure that children have enough to eat, Kiyana (age 12, black British, working lone mother, inner London) says:

'It depends. Cos you never know if it's like they [families] don't get enough money, so then it's not their fault. But then like if they've spent all their money on stuff that they don't really need, it is their fault…Like if you've given money to someone or something like that, but they didn't need it like as much as you need it, then it's both of their faults.'

Likewise, Fahad (age 13, British Asian, lone mother in work, inner London) mentions that the government should help people who are in food poverty but that this does not exempt people from being responsible for themselves:

'Well there's like the government who are like…if they don't have enough food it's obviously their fault for spending their money on stuff like they may not need like and like are not necessary…but like also people feel like the government for not giving them enough money, and the money that they need or what they deserve.'

Phoebe, from the middle class family in the study, says that school and government should both take responsibility when people are in food poverty. In her view, schools should provide free meals and fruit. However, she also invokes individual responsibility:

'So if a family is unable to provide food then I think it's up to schools and government to kind of make that up, if there is really nothing that they can do. So free school meals and fruit at break I think is really important. But at the same time I think people need to be sensible with what they spend, instead of buying a new pair of trainers like providing food for a week. I still find it amazing how people can have like amazing shoes and look amazing, but kind of be malnourished and not eating the right things. But I think it's really important that there is enough money for schools to be able to provide free school meals, breakfast club and fruit and stuff like that.'

Other children suggest that parents ought to act in concert with government and schools to ensure that children do not go without good food that will keep them 'healthy'. Kiyana says:

'Your parents and the government. Cos the government should know like if the children are healthy and that. And your parents just like want you to stay healthy, they don't want you to be unhealthy and like have an illness or something like that.'

Murad (age 12, black British, lone mother on benefits, inner London) suggests that parents, the school and children should all work together to make sure children eat healthily:

'I think it's up to both of them, all three of them. Because if like one doesn't cooperate like let's say the parent doesn't cooperate, the parent doesn't buy salad and fruit, then the child won't have salad and fruit. If the school doesn't cooperate and don't provide salad and fruit then the child might not like salad and fruit and won't have it at home.'

Roberta (age 13, European, two parents in work, coastal area) had recently migrated with her family to the UK. She blames the consumerised school food system in Britain. Instead, she recommends the school meals policy in Italy, where *'in school they all have the same thing and they can't choose…they don't pay'*, thereby illustrating the greater importance that some countries place on the state's responsibility for ensuring children are well fed.

Government

About a quarter of the children think that the government should take more responsibility to ensure that families have enough to eat. Bryony (age 13, white British, lone parent reliant on benefits, coastal area) refers to the pressures of bills on families as well as food:

'...cos people have to pay bills and the government know that people have to pay bills. And sometimes they could just take the money out of other people's accounts...and it gets stupid cos if people actually need that money, and they need it for food or something, then it's their fault. And if...for example, that they need the money to get food, and they ain't able to get food, again it's their fault and they need to sort it out...but they (government) don't.'

One boy points to the government's failure to do anything about homeless people. Arun (age 10, British Asian, two parents in work, coastal area) answers the question by talking about his experience of feeding a homeless man in the street. He also talks about the need for money when people live in cities:

'I think the government, basically the government. Because why would they leave people on the street...without food or something. Once we found a man on the street and we gave him a McDonald's...I think it's a bit sad because...I think money is an important thing in here, you basically couldn't live without money if you're living in a city or something.'

Cole (age 14, white British, coastal area) talks about the government having a more general role to play in society. He thinks that everyone should *get a fair bit of it* including families like his own (white British families with both parents in work). His remarks suggest some of the anti-migrant feeling in the coastal area where he lives and the loss of entitlement to housing and so forth on the part of 'the locals'. This was a dominant narrative at the time of the interview in an area where there was wide support for Brexit:

'I think they should be making sure everyone gets a fair bit of it, especially seeing as people from other countries are coming in and getting given most of the money and all the houses from pretty much nothing and people like who live here and earn money have to pay more for them. I think they should be making that more fair of who gets what...because they haven't earned the right to have houses and food and that. I think if anything the people who've been living here longer, earning the money should be given that right to have the houses and food. It doesn't bother me as such. It's just the fact that they haven't earned the right to have all that stuff. Whereas we do earn it, but can't get it, because they've been given it.'

However, some children say that government should step in when parents cannot find work and cannot meet their children's needs. Kasey (age 13, black British) lives with her lone mother. Her mother was in work at the time of her interview but had become a student at the time of Kasey's interview. As a result, the family's income had significantly dropped. Kasey says:

> 'I think the government should help more because especially like…if parents…like my mum she doesn't have a job so she obviously doesn't have much money coming in. Like it's not imp…well it is important to, like, make sure that you fulfil your child's wants and needs, but obviously she needs to focus on the core things like making sure I have clothes, like making sure I have food, and making sure I can like bathe and stuff. So I think they should help more.'

When asked whose responsibility it is to ensure children and families have access to enough good food, Sean (age 14, white British, lone mother on benefits, inner London) suggests that no one is taking responsibility for food poverty:

> 'I think that it should be the government's job, but I don't think there is anyone that takes responsibility over that. I think parents do the best that they can. And you know there's not much you can ask for other than for their best, you know.'

Sean's mother is awaiting the outcome of her application for income support; she is pregnant and has not worked since being a paid carer for her father who died six months ago. She manages to feed the family on a low income by doing a large food shop once a month, when she receives her child benefit, and topping up with items that are discounted at the end of the day at the local Tesco. The children are often fed by their maternal grandmother who lives locally but their mother is also accruing debts on her credit card. Sean's response conveys a sense of powerlessness about government's lack of intervention in the context of parents being left to do 'the best they can'.

Social inequality

Sean, quoted above, is highly critical of the government that he regards as the cause of growing social inequality:

'Yeah, I think it's all down to the government, because they are making life
so hard for people that don't really have money. Like they're making the poor
people poorer and the rich people richer.'

Sean reflects the view that poverty is structural and cannot be addressed
without engaging with the 'problem of riches'.[10]

Faith (age 15, West African, lone father in work, inner London) also
talks at some length about the British class system. In comparison to
some of the views children expressed above about irresponsible spending
on non-essential items, she is particularly insightful about how difficult it is
for lower income parents to make 'sensible' consumption decisions. We
have quoted at length from her interview because she elaborates her
views so clearly:

'I think it's like…we're still living in a world where classes matter, so the upper
class and the lower class. And, like, the upper class get what they want, what
they need. And there's like people who are in the middle class, they're not poor
but they're rich – they're poor, but they also have money to fend for themself.
And then there's the lower class people, who have a little bit of money but that
money is used for stuff which are important, and not stuff which the children
want. So, like, for instance the child will want something, like buying a new pair
of shoes that their friends have, a new game or a new phone or something that
their friends have…but because the parents feel like the money they have
should go to a good use, like buy them food or buy them clothes that they will
wear for now. Cos like for me, a girl like me, who want…like because my
friends, they wear designer stuff, so I would obviously want designer stuff… but
my dad will obviously (inaudible) "no, I'm not going to buy designer stuff, I'll buy
you normal clothes so that you use to shelter yourself for now, you know". A
lot of those people they think…they use the money for something useful, not
what the kids want. And the middle class people they just…they have money
so they're able to use the money to buy for what they think is important and
what the child needs. And then the upper class people, they do everything.'

Faith articulates very clearly the context of children's need to keep up with
their friends and the consequences for children in low-income families
who come off worse than their better-off peers. She goes on to extrapolate about the feelings that social inequality engenders among people living
in poverty and asserts the right to be, and to feel, equal:

'I think like everyone should be classified as equal, everyone shouldn't be…
like, for instance, if you are a lower class person and you walk into a place

full of everyone there, you shouldn't feel as if you're out of place – which nor-
mally they feel. So you shouldn't feel as if you're out of the place, you feel as
if you belong there – the clothes you're wearing are up to the standards, the
food you eat are the same food (they) you eat. And if you want to go out
you're able to go out with them and spend the amount of money you want
with them, like they are doing…but you can't do that.'

A key aspect of social inclusion in Faith's view is being able to live according to the normative expectations of the society, including for everyone to
be able to eat 'the same food'.

Summary

These young people are at a critical phase in their lives, a time when they
are forging their separate identities as individuals. Poverty, and food
poverty in particular, are potentially shaming experiences that affect how
children and young people see themselves and how they position themselves in relation to their peers.

Despite parents' attempts to protect children from going without
food, most children seem aware of the financial and food constraints that
their families face. Some suggest that they conceal the potentially shaming experiences from others. In this way, they can avoid being publicly
shamed and lessen the internalised experience of feeling shame. Others
are resilient and positive. Some defend themselves against being labelled
'poor' and consider their families better off than others. Others are proactive in helping their families to get by, for example, by saving food or hunting for bargains.

Some children speak eloquently about the shame of being looked
down upon by others: in having to resort to food banks, in not being able
to offer hospitality to their friends, for having supermarket 'value' foods.
One girl also speaks at length about the social class system that she
regards as lying at the root of inequalities in income and consumption.

Questions about whose responsibility it is to ensure that children are
fed enable young people to externalise the 'problem'. Children place the
moral responsibility for poverty, and food poverty in particular, in large
measure at the door of government when families experience periods of
hardship. At the same time, they take it almost as a given that, under normal conditions, parents are charged with ensuring that their children are
adequately fed. However, children also assert that people are responsible

for managing their lives and that parents should prioritise essential expenditure and not waste money on less important things. Young people use and reproduce discourses about individual responsibility and, occasionally seek to distinguish themselves from 'others' who are seen as lacking entitlement. Overall, responsibility for ensuring children's access to adequate food is considered to lie with government but with parents and schools too.

Notes

1   J Brannen, K Dodd, A Oakley and P Storey, *Young People, Health and Family Life,* Open University Press, 1994. These authors found that young people gave rosier evaluations of their 'health' (broadly defined) in interviews than in questionnaires.

2   E Goffman, *Stigma: notes on the management of spoiled identity*, Penguin Books, 1974, p122

3   UKIP – the UK Independence Party – was instrumental in bringing about the referendum on leaving the European Union.

4   N Smith and S Middleton, *A Review of Poverty Dynamics Research in the UK*, Joseph Rowntree Foundation, 2007

5   See also K Hill and A Davis, *Making Ends Meet Below the Minimum Income Standard: families' experiences over time*, CRSP Working Paper 662, Centre for Research in Social Policy, 2018, p14

6   AJ Pugh, *Longing and Belonging: parents, children, and consumer culture*, University of California Press, 2009

7   A Phoenix, *Review of Recent Literature for the Bailey Review of Commercialisation and Sexualisation of Childhood: a review by the Childhood Wellbeing Research Centre*, CWRC Working Paper No.2, Childhood Wellbeing Research Centre, 2011, p24

8   A Phoenix, 'Young people and consumption: commonalities and differences in the construction of identities', in B Tufte, J Rasmussen and LB Christensen (eds), *Frontrunners or copycats?*, Copenhagen Business School Press, 2005, pp78–98

9   A Marsh, K Barker, C Ayrton, M Treanor and M Haddad, *Poverty: the facts*, Child Poverty Action Group, 2017, Chapter 11

10 R Tawney, 'Poverty as an industrial problem', inaugural lecture, reproduced in *Memoranda on the Problems of Poverty*, William Morris Press, 1913. Tawney argued that 'what thoughtful rich people call the problem of poverty, thoughtful poor people call with equal justice a problem of riches' (p10).

Nine

Summing up and recommendations

Children in low-income families are at constant risk of poor nutrition and denied participation in many of the everyday activities enjoyed by their peers. Their experiences of living on a low income include hunger, social exclusion and endlessly juggling insufficient money to meet their material and social needs. This also means managing painful feelings of shame and embarrassment about their situations. While children take for granted that parents are primarily responsible for feeding their families, they acknowledge that they cannot always manage this, despite doing their best. Some children blame social inequality and identify a role for schools and government in helping children and families who are struggling.

There is considerable variation in children's experiences. However, the opportunities available to young people turn on the source, size and continuity of parents' income – from the labour market, the state and charity. They also depend upon the policies of the state, specifically relating to immigration and benefit levels and entitlement, and the policies and practices of the schools they attend. The types of communities in which they live also have significant effects on young people. Of particular relevance to food is the consumerism to which childhood is subject that is reflected in the wide availability of fast food outlets and their attractiveness to growing teenagers with little money to spend. In the inner London borough, increasing gentrification means that young people are excluded from the new 'café culture' that is taking over former working class high streets, while, in the coastal area, expensive public transport restricts children's opportunities for meeting and eating with their friends.

Despite the constraints young people encountered, they demonstrated considerable resourcefulness and resilience. They developed an active relationship with their living conditions that was reflected in the resources – both internal and external – that children mobilised, the strategies they deployed in their mobilisation, and the meanings they attributed both to the experiences of food and food poverty and to their lives more generally.

One sign of young people's resilience that we have not yet touched upon in the book concerns how they perceive the future. The final section

reflects upon some of the children's views about their futures and our recommendations for what might be done to improve children's and families'
future access to sufficient food for health and social inclusion.

How do young people feel about the future?

One hundred years ago, Maud Pember Reeves placed the blame for
underfed school children firmly on the government's doorstep.[1] In Britain
today, the problem of want among plenty is as pervasive as ever. We are
living through a period of deep political and economic uncertainty. Leaving
the European Union and the accompanying Brexit negotiations, further
cuts to welfare benefits alongside continued stagnation in wages, higher
inflation, including food prices, and stringent immigration control currently
make for a gloomy prospect. The plight of young people and families like
those in this book looks unlikely to improve.

Asked about the future, a number of young people spoke about the
future in general. They expressed concern about further benefit cuts, citizens not being cared for, the rising cost of living, food access and the
health of children. But when asked about their own futures, in general they
were positive and ambitious. Some focused on the present or next phase
in their lives: getting good GCSE grades, going to sixth form college, the
subjects they would like to study, and going to university. Those who
thought further ahead talked about getting 'good jobs' and fending for
their families, while others mentioned specific careers – including being a
footballer and a police officer. One young man whose family members
were asylum seekers awaiting appeal said he wanted to be *'an advocate
or an ambassador, yeah, just want to help people, cos I just love doing
that'*. But perhaps most illuminating are the words of Amara, age 15, who,
with her mother, is dependent on charity, living in a hostel and waiting eviction. She articulates with great poignancy how she came to Britain to get
an education but feels caught in an uncertain present:

> '...if I'm in this country, I'm here for a reason; I'm here because my mum
> wants to give me a good education, and that's what I'm doing, I'm studying
> hard[.] I'm doing my best to get good grades. And then once I finish I'm
> going to go college, and if God knows and I do have enough money, I'm
> going to university then [...] see what I really want to do in life. [...] But I can't
> focus on the future if I don't know what's going to happen from now till...like
> from now to the next hour. I can't just go like [...] I can't, I need to think about

now, like think about the present. Then one day the future will come and we'll see what happens. But I have plans for the future, I mean, I will study, I will do my best to get my grades and just have a good job, and not end up being poor and asking people for help. I want to be the man of the house. I mean having a job, taking care of my mum.'

Recommendations on dignity and human rights

'My social worker, she gave my mum some food voucher to the [food bank in the] church by Lidl's. And they gave us like noodles, like tins of tomatoes and beans. We still have some in the cupboard. They gave us like spaghetti and stuff, and they gave us cereal and biscuits…and they gave us some dilute juice. […] we prayed…no we waited, then we prayed, then we got the food, then we went to the sermon […] It wasn't really…I don't know how to explain it…it wasn't on like…I don't know how to word it now…oh I forgot the word, I just had it in my head […] Like it wasn't really an atmosphere I would feel comfortable around.' (Kasey, age 13, black British, inner London)

The current situation in Britain is one in which public policy and the media blame individuals for their plight while leaving the response to food poverty to charity and giving 'wasted food to surplus people'.[2] As the book has shown, food adequacy is about much more than nutritional intake. This means that minimalist approaches to defining need and responses must be challenged. Food banks and food charity cannot 'solve' the problem of food poverty and, in fact, may serve to stigmatise and marginalise further those already suffering material deprivation and social exclusion. People should have the right to food, not to be fed.

We recommend the following.

- Tangible steps should be taken nationally to facilitate the progressive realisation of the right to food, beginning with a consultation on the 'right to food'.[3]
- The government should establish and fund a regular systematic measure of food poverty in the UK that includes children.
- All children should have a right to a basic standard of living (with reference to the Minimum Income Standard – MIS), with an adequate family income to provide autonomy and choice, particularly in relation to family diet and adequacy of food.
- Emergency food charities should expand their advocacy and cam-

paigning role in speaking to wider political processes and addressing the structural determinants of food poverty, such as problems with the social security system.

- Crisis response services and local welfare assistance schemes should aim, wherever possible, to provide cash-based responses to food poverty to enable children and families to make their own cultural choices in relation to food.

Recommendations on employment and benefits

'I don't know it's kind of like parents' [responsibility to make sure the family eats well] isn't it, but then parents can't really supply you with food if they don't have like a good job, like good work and pay. So it's kind of like parents plus like job people like…I don't know what you call them, like managers or whatever.' (Charlie, age 15 white British, inner London)

In some European countries, investment in welfare successfully removes families from poverty. But central to UK policy is an emphasis on paid employment. However, lone parents' employment opportunities are constrained by high childcare costs and low-paid part-time work. Moreover, the largest proportion (two-thirds) of households with children living in relative poverty in the UK includes at least one employed adult, suggesting that paid work does not provide a route out of poverty.

Universal credit is meant to address these issues and 'make work pay'. However, its implementation has had a devastating effect on many families and, as this book has shown, families whose benefits are being reassessed may be left with nothing for weeks at a time. In these circumstances, child benefit provides a vital lifeline.

The real cost of raising a child and feeding a family is calculated annually by researchers at the Centre for Research in Social Policy at Loughborough University. The same team calculates Joseph Rowntree Foundation's MIS. MIS is used to determine the 'real living wage',[4] which is based on what people need to live.

We recommend the following.

- Food poverty is a result of inadequate income, not a shortage of food. All children should grow up in a household with an adequate income to afford a healthy and balanced diet.
- Government policy should use MIS research to ensure that wages

and welfare benefits, in combination, are adequate for a socially acceptable standard of living and eating that recognises the fundamental role of food in health and social inclusion.

- A labour market strategy is required which gives employees greater security – for example, by ending zero-hour contracts and offering minimum-hour contracts.
- Employers should be encouraged to pay the real living wage.
- Social security support for children and families should be actively promoted to prevent poverty and protect the vulnerable, including refugees and asylum seekers.
- The freeze on benefits for working-age people should be lifted and benefits should be uprated annually.
- Child benefit, a universal benefit aimed at meeting the needs of children, is set to lose 24 per cent of its value between 2010 and 2020[5] – it should be uprated by £5 a week per child to restore its value.
- The well-documented failings in universal credit require immediate reform before more families with children are moved on to universal credit.
- The benefit cap, that is increasing child poverty by breaking the link between a family's needs and the support received, should be abolished. It discriminates particularly against lone parents and their children who are more likely to be capped and less able to avoid its impact because of their caring responsibilities.
- The 'two-child limit' in tax credits and universal credit, that will push a further 200,000 children into poverty, should be abolished.

Recommendations on immigration policy

'Yeah like Year 7 yeah, we used to like eat. But now in Year 8, 9, 10 we haven't eaten cos my mum's stopped working, not enough food coming… we have to like cope with what…not spend nothing cos like if you do then we're going to struggle even more, so…' (Gideon, age 15, West African, inner London, whose mother's 'limited leave to remain' has expired)

Mounting evidence suggests that welfare and immigration policies are a major cause of insecurity and precarity for those subject to Home Office control. Welfare support has been increasingly withheld by successive governments from migrant groups without leave to remain as a tool for controlling immigration. This is creating hunger among children and families who have no recourse to public funds, leaving them totally dependent on charity. A 2015 study from the University of Oxford's Centre on Migration, Policy and Society (COMPAS) estimated that, in 2012/13, there were around 3,400 families and 5,900 children with no recourse to public funds whose basic needs were being met by local authorities.[6] However, research from the Children's Society[7] suggests that the numbers in need may be greater, since only 38 per cent of families who apply for this support from local authorities receive it.[8] As the migrant mothers we interviewed said, they did not want to be dependent on benefits or charity; having a job was a matter of pride in caring for their families.

We recommend the following.

- Since the government shares a duty to care for children with parents, it should give all parents, including migrants, 'recourse to public funds' if they have children under 18 years old.[9]
- Because children whose parents have no recourse to public funds are not entitled to free school meals (FSMs), they go hungry at school as well as at home. Making FSMs universal would solve this problem. In the meantime, the Education Act 1996 should be amended to ensure that children in families that have no recourse to public funds are entitled to receive FSMs.

Recommendations on school policies

'So, when she [lunchtime staff at the checkout] was like, "You can't get that, you're free school meals", like I was really embarrassed cos people were waiting behind me, I was kind of like "Oh my God". And I was like, "But I've technically got £2 on my account", she was like, "No you can't get that at free school meals". And it's like you're really restricted to what you can eat with free school meals. And it's like if you're saying £2 is on my balance surely I should be able to get something that's worth less than £2. So that really like got me, so now I just get what I know I'm safe with…so a small baguette and carton of juice.' (Maddy, age 16, white British, inner London)

Schools are insufficiently resourced and cannot be expected to solve the problems caused by the retrenchment of the welfare state. However, they are well placed to identify which children are in need and their practices can, and do, both reduce and compound social inequalities.

Nutritious school meals are essential for children's health and an important means of their socialisation and inclusion. However, national policies and local practices often fall short. A large number of children in low-income working families are, or will become, ineligible for FSMs. Government should extend, not reduce, entitlement to FSMs in order to eliminate social stigma and fragmentation as well as nutritional and health inequalities.

Significant resources are being invested in non-statutory interventions before and after school and in school holidays. Extended schools are an important source of childcare and food provision for working families, while school holiday programmes can provide meals for children who would otherwise go without.

We recommend the following.

- Reduced eligibility for FSMs reflects a rise in in-work poverty: FSMs should no longer be used as a proxy for school children growing up in poverty.
- School meals should be free for all children at school and be provided as part of the normal school day, without stigma or means-testing.
- In the meantime, the delivery of FSMs should be 'shame-proofed'[10] in education legislation in all parts of the UK, as they are in Wales and Scotland.
- Children, young people and staff, especially lunchtime staff, have important roles to play in improving children's experiences of school food. Lunchtime staffing should be properly funded with both staff and children being meaningfully involved in making mealtimes enjoyable, healthier and more inclusive.
- School food standards are not mandatory in all schools in England and implementation is patchy. There is also a mismatch between food availability and the formal curriculum. This needs to be addressed to make all schools in the UK 'healthy food' zones.[11]
- Revenue gained through the sugar (or other) tax should be used to fund extended school activities both before and after school and throughout school holidays.
- Extended schools provision and schemes aimed at tackling holiday hunger should be universal and inclusive, located in existing extended schools facilities that children and families know and trust. Integrating meals and snacks with activities will help ease the burden on parents without the risk of the stigma associated with food banks and other food crisis services.
- Fresh fruit and vegetables should be provided in school food and

extended school activities to reduce inequalities in access to the health benefits of a balanced diet.

- To support families to maximise their income, welfare rights advice services should be provided and located alongside extended school provision or another convenient community location.

Recommendations on children's spaces and the food environment

'There are times when you want to keep yourself to yourself…if you're angry or upset…but like you see your mum and she's crying, you don't want to be alone with her, but there's nowhere else to go. So…' (Shola, age 14, West African, living with her mother and brother in one room of a shared house)

Inadequate housing, expensive public transport, lack of money and safe places to play or hang out constrain children's opportunities for socialising. In these conditions, fast food outlets are an important place for young people to meet and buy cheap food that they enjoy. However, their prevalence in deprived neighbourhoods has been linked to health inequalities while young people are targeted by manufacturers of high fat, salt or sugar products.

We recommend the following.

- The number of families in temporary accommodation has risen by 62 per cent since 2010.[12] Government should support local councils' efforts to reduce homelessness by allowing them to invest in building genuinely affordable homes and by taking steps to ensure that new and existing stock is affordable for low-income families.
- Young people lack places and opportunities to socialise. There should be a statutory duty to provide sustainable funding for youth services and young people should be involved and consulted about youth service provision in their local areas. Fair pay for youth workers is needed.
- Public transport should be free (or more accessible and affordable) for children outside of London to ease financial pressures on families and reduce social isolation and exclusion.
- Regulations on advertising of less healthy food products and the soft drinks industry levy have been welcomed by children's heath campaigners. But further action – restrictions on pricing, advertising

and planning – needs to be taken to improve the local food environment as well as the promotion of unhealthy foods targeted at young people.

Notes

1 M Pember Reeves, *Round about a Pound a Week,* Persephone Books, 1913

2 G Riches and T Silvasti (eds), *First World Hunger Revisited: food charity or the right to food?*, Palgrave Macmillan, 2014; H Lambie-Mumford, *Hungry Britain: the rise of food charity*, Policy Press, 2017

3 H Lambie-Mumford, *Hungry Britain: The Rise of Food Charity*, Policy Press, 2017

4 Living Wage Foundation, Citizens UK

5 Child Poverty Action Group, *The Austerity Generation: the impact of a decade of cuts on family incomes and child poverty*, November 2017

6 J Price and S Spencer, *Safeguarding children from destitution: local authority responses to families with 'no recourse to public funds'*, COMPAS, 2015, available at www.compas.ox.ac.uk/wp-content/uploads/PR-2015-No_Recourse_Public_Funds_LAs.pdf

7 Z Dexter, L Capron and L Gregg, *Making Life Impossible: how the needs of destitute migrant children are going unmet,* The Children's Society, 2016

8 L Partridge, *The Hidden Poverty in our schools*, RSA blog at www.thersa.org/discover/publications-and-articles/rsa-blogs/2018/07/hidden-poverty-in-our-schools

9 See note 7, p34

10 R Walker, 'Preface' in EK Gubrium, S Pellisser and I Lødemel (eds), *The Shame of It*, Policy Press, 2014, pxxiii.

11 Sustain, *Sustain and Children's Food Campaign's submission to the Health Select Committee Inquiry on government progress against the Childhood Obesity Plan*, 2018 at http://data.parliament.uk/writtenevidence/committeeevidence.svc/evidencedocument/health-and-social-care-committee/childhood-obesity/written/81225.pdf

12 'The rising number of homeless children in the UK explained', 20 April 2018, inews, https://inews.co.uk/news/uk/figures-behind-child-homelessness-explained/; 'The living conditions of London's most disadvantaged children', BBC News, 5 December 2018, www.bbc.co.uk/news/in-pictures-46344967

Appendix 1
Methodology and sample

Table 1.1

Lone and dual parent households in the inner London borough and coastal town (N=45)

	Lone parent	Dual parent	Total
Inner city area	23	7	30
Coastal town	7	8	15
Total	30	15	45

Table 1.2

Families by quintile[1] (N=45)

	Household income quintile (equivalised after housing costs)			
Source of income	One	Two	Three	Total (N=45)
A: At least one adult in paid work	9	13	3	25
B: Benefits only	8	7	1	16
C: No work, no benefits	4	0	0	4
Total (N=45)	21	20	4	45

1　Equivalised household income after housing costs was calculated and compared to the national distribution in the *Households Below Average Income* (HBAI) statistics for 2016/17 (the fieldwork years) (see Appendix 2).

Table 1.3

Mother's ethnicity/country of origin in the inner London borough and coastal area (N=45)

	Inner London borough	Coastal area	Total
White British	7	8	15
Black British	7	0	7
British Asian	4	0	4
Asian	0	1	1
European	0	2	2
Eastern European	2	3	5
West African	9	1	10
North African	1	0	1
Total	**30**	**15**	**45**

Appendix 2
Calculating equivalised income (quintiles)

Equivalisation adjusts household income to account for the different financial resource requirements of different household types. In order to make meaningful comparisons between the income distribution of the sample and the national context, as well as cross nationally in the wider study, we have calculated equivalised income.

Equivalisation can be applied to income before or after housing costs and there are advantages and disadvantages of each. Because of the variability in the way housing costs are met (eg, directly by households, through the benefits system, by subsidised housing, or a combination of these), we have equivalised after housing costs (AHC).[1] Once equivalised household income AHC has been calculated, this can be compared to national data (using the same methodology) about income distribution for the relevant years.

In the UK, the Households Below Average Income (HBAI) dataset provides official statistics on poverty and the distribution of household income. The data are based on the Family Resources Survey. The HBAI uses modified Organisation for Economic Co-operation and Development (OECD) equivalisation scales for calculating income before and after housing costs.[2]

In the UK, we have used the modified OECD methodology to calculate the equivalised income AHC for households in the qualitative sample. We have compared this to the statistics for 2015/2016[3] to give the income quintile for each household.

The modified OECD 'companion' scale to equivalise AHC results is shown in Table 2.1.

Results

In the UK we found that the sample was fairly evenly distributed between the lowest two income quintiles, with a few families in the middle income quintile. Note that one of these families has children with disabilities – given equivalisation scales do not allow for additional needs their 'real' equivalised income is likely much lower.

When we looked at equivalised income by type of income we found that in the lowest income quintile about as many families had at least one adult in paid work as were on benefits only, while in the second lowest income quintile around twice as many families had at least one adult in paid work as were on benefits only (Table 2.2).

Table 2.1

Modified OECD companion scale used to calculate income after housing costs

	Equivalence value
First adult	0.58
Spouse	0.42
Other second adult	0.42
Third adult	0.42
Subsequent adults	0.42
Children aged under 14 years	0.20
Children aged 14 years and over	0.42

Table 2.2

Equivalised Income (AHC) quintile by income type (N=45)

Work code	Household income quintile (equivalised after housing costs)			
	One	Two	Three	Total (N=45)
A: At least one adult in paid work	9	13	3	25
B: Benefits only	8	7	1	16
C: No work, no benefits	4	0	0	4
Total (N=45)	**21**	**20**	**4**	**45**

Notes

1 These are crude estimates as it is difficult to collect accurate income as part of a longer interview and income may fluctuate. Also, we did not collect some housing costs – eg, home insurance.

2 HBAI uses modified OECD equivalisation scales for before and after housing costs. Methodology for this (sort of) is explained at www.gov.uk/government/uploads/system/uploads/attachment_data/file/599163/households-below-average-income-quality-metholodogy-2015-2016.pdf.

3 The tables are available at www.gov.uk/government/statistics/households-below-average-income-199495-to-201516 under the supporting data tables heading. Median income (before and after housing costs) is given for all years going back to 1994/95 in the latest year's prices (so for this year is 2015/16).